Secrets
of Wine

52 Brilliant Ideas

one good idea can change your life

Secrets of Wine

Know Your Cab from Your Merlot— Without the Terroir

Giles Kime

A Perigee Book

A PERIGEE BOOK
Published by the Penguin Group
Penguin Group (USA) Inc.
375 Hudson Street, New York, New York 10014, USA
Penguin Group (Canada), 90 Eglinton Avenue East, Suite 700, Toronto, Ontario M4P 2Y3, Canada
(a division of Pearson Penguin Canada Inc.)
Penguin Books Ltd., 80 Strand, London WC2R 0RL, England
Penguin Group Ireland, 25 St. Stephen's Green, Dublin 2, Ireland (a division of Penguin Books Ltd.)
Penguin Group (Australia), 250 Camberwell Road, Camberwell, Victoria 3124, Australia
(a division of Pearson Australia Group Pty. Ltd.)
Penguin Books India Pvt. Ltd., 11 Community Centre, Panchsheel Park, New Delhi—110 017, India
Penguin Group (NZ), 67 Apollo Drive, Rosedale, North Shore 0745, Auckland, New Zealand
(a division of Pearson New Zealand Ltd.)
Penguin Books (South Africa) (Pty.) Ltd., 24 Sturdee Avenue, Rosebank, Johannesburg 2196, South Africa

Penguin Books Ltd., Registered Offices: 80 Strand, London WC2R 0RL, England

SECRETS OF WINE

Copyright © 2005 by The Infinite Ideas Company Limited
Cover art by Lucy Dickens
Text design by Baseline Arts Ltd., Oxford

First American edition: July 2007
Originally published in Great Britain in 2005 by The Infinite Ideas Company Limited.

Perigee trade paperback ISBN: 978-0-399-53348-8

PRINTED IN THE UNITED STATES OF AMERICA

10   9   8   7   6   5   4   3   2   1

Brilliant ideas

Brilliant features

Each chapter of this book is designed to provide you with an inspirational idea that you can read quickly and put into practice right away.

Throughout you'll find four features that will help you to get right to the heart of the idea:

- *Here's an idea for you* Give it a try—right here, right now—and get an idea of how well you're doing so far.

- *Try another idea* If this idea looks like a life-changer then there's no time to lose. *Try another idea* will point you straight to a related tip to expand and enhance the first.

- *Defining ideas* Words of wisdom from masters and mistresses of the art, plus some interesting hangers-on.

- *How did it go?* If at first you do succeed, try to hide your amazement. If, on the other hand, you don't, this is where you'll find a Q and A that highlights common problems and how to get over them.

Introduction

A wine bore is someone whose head is full of other people's ideas. A free-thinking drinker is one whose head is full of his own. In showing you how to become the latter this book will allow you to achieve vinous nirvana.

You can never really hope to learn anything about a subject simply by reading. That is the reason the best books are those that equip you with the skills to make your own discoveries, develop opinions, and deepen your understanding. For the uninitiated, there are few things quite as subjective as wine. If you are told that a wine is grassy, the chances are that grassiness is what you'll find. If you are told that it is fruity, then you'll make it conform to some stereotype of fruitiness in your head. Unlike every other book written on wine this one won't tell you what you should think about a wine. It will simply provide you with the skills you need to make up your own mind.

To become a free-thinking drinker you don't need fancy equipment and a library of reference books, just . . .

- some very large, deep, tulip-shaped wineglasses with fine rims
- a knowledgeable wine merchant with whom you can develop a meaningful, lifelong relationship
- self-adhesive labels to indicate the identity of wines
- crackers to purge the palate
- a spittoon—a Champagne bucket is ideal
- a notebook to write your observations in
- a good wine atlas
- an open mind

TASTE YOUR WAY TO THE TOP

Extensive tasting is the only way you'll ever deepen your understanding of wine. Great tasters are not necessarily people who are born with a special gift; they are simply people who are lucky enough to have had the opportunity to taste a great many wines at the same time. Anyone who spent an afternoon in a room full of Chardonnays would be amazed how quickly they'd be able to identify different characters in the wines and to guess successfully where they came from.

However, tasting in a random way has only a limited use. Whenever necessary, there is a suggestion for a taste test that will enable you to compare one style of wine with another in a focused way. It is these differences—sometimes elusive, sometimes obvious—that over time will help you define the character of a wine and build up a database of flavors and aromas in your head.

What is crucial to these tests is anonymity. Only when you have thoroughly examined every conceivable shade of difference between the wines should you reveal their identity. This second stage will offer yet another layer of interest.

Ideally, all the wines should be tasted in one sitting. If the wines are expensive it makes financial sense to share the tasting with another curious wine enthusiast. But remember, you don't need to drink the wines at one sitting—most wine will keep for up to three days (and even longer if sealed under pressure in a preserving system). Conducting the test before and during a meal will allow you to taste wine as part of a greater gastronomic experience—which in most cases is just as the winemaker intended—and will significantly enhance your enjoyment of the wine.

Because the availability of some wines is so patchy—and because many change from one year to the next—the suggestions are kept deliberately vague, e.g., cheap Australian Cabernet, good-quality white Burgundy. This is where a good wine merchant comes in. You need to find one who can understand what you are looking for and will then come up with a wine that is typical.

What you won't find in this book is any discussion of how one wine tasted against another. The wines rather than the words are intended to speak for themselves.

1

Never mind the bollocks

If you open a bottle of wine burdened with preconceived ideas based on its label, its price, and myths spun by the wine trade, it's time to learn the art of free-thinking drinking.

The premise of most books on wine is that the path to vinous enlightenment is fathomless depths of knowledge.

The theory goes like this: In order to truly understand wine you must have a good understanding of geography (so that you can find your way around a map of every wine region from Bordeaux to the Barossa), geology (to understand the effect that ferruginous oolite found in Burgundy's soil can have on the flavor of a glass of Volnay), and chemistry (for those fascinating late-night discussions about malolactic fermentation). A working knowledge of meteorology, the French language, and European wine law might also come in handy.

Authors of wine books expect their readers to become receptacles for reams of facts and secondhand opinions. For most readers, all this is in addition to the weight of misconceptions that they have picked up from the wine trade, the media, and the droves of oenophiles who are so generous with their spurious views on wine.

Here's an idea for you...

The next time you open a bottle of wine, plot its origin as precisely as you can. You will find that rooting a wine in a particular part of the globe will give the wine a context that makes it easier to understand.

THE MINISTERS OF MISINFORMATION

Though obfuscation hasn't been a deliberate policy pursued by those in the wine trade, it has certainly helped them to charge high prices for perfectly ordinary wines. In Bordeaux, for example, there is a complex league table of chateaux known as the Grand Cru Classés that consists of five different divisions. Although the chateaux are within a few miles of one another, a wine from the first division can be priced as much as 300 percent higher than one from the fifth. Is this because a wine in the first division is 300 percent better? No, it's because this is the way that the wines were graded in the mid-nineteenth century and the pecking order has remained the same ever since.

Bordeaux is not the only wine region in which these hierarchies exist. They can be found all over Europe and do nothing but confuse the consumer and bolster complacent producers. If you need more convincing, you need only look at the numerous blind tastings in which supermarket Champagnes trounce those that sell for three to four times the price or landmark tastings such as the one held in Paris in 1976, which ranked some wines from California—then a Johnny-come-lately of the wine world—above some of Bordeaux's finest.

Many wine producers—especially those at the top end of the market—must have realized that confusion (or "mystique" as they prefer to call it) can be used to commercial advantage. This means that selling wine is not like selling cornflakes, a commodity on which most people can put a value. A bottle of wine can be sold for twice the amount of something comparable purely because it has a certain name or year on its label. Sadly, the result of mystique is likely to be disheartened customers whose initial enthusiasm for wine is dampened by the fact that they can't remember the names of the top wines in the 1855 classification of Bordeaux or don't have an intimate knowledge of the topography of the Mosel Valley.

In IDEA 21, *Bordeaux, Burgundy, and Champagne,* you're invited to explore the question of whether some wines—particularly French ones—are all mouth and no trousers.

Try another idea...

THREE STEPS TO VINOUS ENLIGHTENMENT

- *Question everything.* Don't accept anyone's word for anything. Most people who claim to be wine experts base their opinions on where a wine comes from, when it was made, and what they have read about it. Just because a wine is served with great aplomb in a restaurant doesn't mean that you have to like it—though it's up to you whether you decide to express your opinion, particularly if someone else is paying.

- *Drink everything.* The fact that you don't like a wine doesn't mean you shouldn't taste it. The more wines you taste, whether good or bad, the greater your frame of reference. However, for the sake of your liver, remember that there's a crucial difference between tasting and drinking.

- *Compare everything.* A wine is defined by how it is similar to, or different from, another. It is these subtle shades of difference—between, say, an inexpensive red Bordeaux and a Chilean Merlot, an Australian sparkling wine and a bottle of vintage Champagne, a Macon and a Chablis—that will reveal the true character of a wine.

"The only means of strengthening one's intellect is to make up one's mind about nothing–to let the mind be a thoroughfare for all thought."
JOHN KEATS

Defining idea...

3

Q **So is a knowledge of geology, geography, and chemistry unnecessary to the aspiring wine buff?**

A *In the same way that a knowledge of the principles of the internal combustion engine will help you understand a car, a rudimentary understanding of how grapes turn into wine is handy. But go any deeper than that and you may soon get bogged down in detail.*

Q **But doesn't it help to know where wine comes from?**

A *Indeed. I'd recommend that you never taste wine without a wine atlas at hand. Wine buffs who rejoice in becoming founts of knowledge seem to forget that there's nothing about geography—or geology and chemistry for that matter—that you can't look up.*

2
The agony of choice

When Isaiah Berlin famously moaned about "the agony of choice" he might have just visited a wine merchant. But, however wide the choice of wines on sale, only a relatively small number need to concern the free-thinking drinker.

"Mystique" isn't the only thing that inhibits the fledgling wine lover. We've all had that sinking feeling when staring at the shelves of a wine store. Even those with a limited range offer wines from the four corners of the earth.

Besides wines from the obvious places such as France, Spain, and Italy, there will be bottles from Greece, Moldova, Morocco, Uruguay, Tasmania, Washington, Oregon. Then there are the grape varieties. For most people Cabernet, Merlot, Pinot Noir, Chardonnay, and Sauvignon Blanc have a familiar ring, but what about Gewürztraminer, Gruner Veltliner, Sangiovese, Tannat?

The world of wine was once a much smaller place. Though wine has been made in Australia since the 1780s, the industry as we know it today wasn't born until the '50s

Here's an idea for you... **Take a scarily long list from your wine retailer and try to "weed" it with a thick black marker—by crossing out either everything except for Bordeaux, Burgundy, the Loire, Australia, and New Zealand or everything that isn't labeled Cabernet Sauvignon, Merlot, Pinot Noir, Sauvignon Blanc, or Chardonnay. Suddenly the list looks less scary, doesn't it?**

and it wasn't until the '80s that good Australian wines became widely available beyond the Antipodes. Before the arrival of such a vast array of wines on merchants' shelves, wine appreciation was a simpler, more focused business, encompassing little more than Bordeaux, Burgundy, German whites, Champagne, and Port.

The problem today is the belief among wine experts that we should see the good in *everything*. "You'd be wrong to dismiss the wines of Transylvania," you hear them drawl. "I recently tasted a delicious late-harvest Riesling that proves they have the potential to produce excellent wines." So they drone on, extolling the virtues of wines from every obscure wine-making region.

THE SECRET OF WEEDING

One of the secrets of free-thinking drinking is to start by reducing the number of wines in your radar. It's similar to the approach taken by a friend of mine to deal with hefty weekend newspapers. She carries out a ruthless process she refers to as "paper weeding." First to be thrown in the trash are the leaflets advertising garden furniture, then the finance and business sections, and finally the sports section—which leaves her with the news, arts, and the comics. Graduates of business school now refer to such a strategy as "starting macro and going micro" (a philosophy that past generations might have described as "not biting off more than you can chew").

A similar approach can be applied to all sorts of subjects. For many people, a first introduction to the vast subject of painting, drawing, and sculpture is *The Story of Art* by Ernst Gombrich. This excellent book is far from being a dumbed-down tour of its subject. Instead, it gives the reader a new way of looking at fine art through the work of the key artists. For many art historians, this book has provided an entry point into a fascinating world.

Try another idea...

The concept that wine is primarily the product of the earth and the weather rather than of winemaking is known as "terroir"—a vague term that has no English equivalent. See IDEA 13, *Come rain or shine*, to find out how weather affects wine.

So how do you weed a monster as vast and sprawling as the wine-producing regions? There are two different approaches, one for the classically minded, the other for the modernists. Both cover precisely the same ground but from two different perspectives.

CLASSICAL AND MODERNIST APPROACHES

The classical approach is geographical and encompasses three classic French wine regions—Bordeaux, Burgundy, and the Loire— and two New World regions—Australia and New Zealand. The modernist approach views the subject from the perspective of the world's five most successful grapes: Cabernet Sauvignon, Merlot, Pinot Noir, Sauvignon Blanc, and Chardonnay.

Defining idea...

"There is a misunderstanding among marketers in our culture about what freedom of choice is. In the market, it is equated with multiplying choice. This is a misconception. If you have infinite choice, people are reduced to passivity."
THE NEW YORK TIMES

Neither method is better than the other. The difference is not one of old experts versus revolutionaries, but one of philosophy. Classicists believe that wine is primarily a product of the earth whereas modernists see it as a product of wine-making. There are convincing arguments for both perspectives. The truth, of course, is that wine is a product of both.

Whichever route you choose to follow, a good knowledge of the flavors and aromas associated with either the regions or the grapes will offer foundations on which to build a deeper understanding of wine and give you a key to a greater world beyond. Trust me.

How did it go?

Q Won't the weeding approach to wine appreciation mean that I'll miss out on a lot of weird and wonderful wines?

A   *The idea behind weeding isn't that you only ever drink a handful of different wines. But, initially, it's a good idea to focus on a core of wines. With a solid basis to work from, your first taste of Bulgarian Rkatsiteli or Uruguyan Tannat won't seem quite so terrifying.*

Q Was it easier to be a wine buff before such a wide range of choice arrived on wine merchants' shelves?

A   *Not really, because with fewer wines to choose from, wine buffs took an insanely detailed interest in the smaller number of wines and obsessed about subjects such as the differences between one vintage and another.*

3

The comfort of strangers

The quickest and most effective way to dispose of oenological baggage is to taste wines anonymously.

There is a game that wine merchants of the old school play after lunch—which involves pouring the contents of an unidentified bottle into the glasses of those slumped around the table in postprandial stupor.

The aim is to guess the identity of the wine by means of a sequence of multiple-choice questions that offer increasingly specific options: "Is it French or Australian?," "Bordeaux or Burgundy?," "Margaux or St. Emilion?," and so on until someone identifies the chateau where it was made.

Such highjinks are guaranteed to strike fear into the heart of anyone who has only just mastered the knack of telling a Chardonnay from a Sauvignon. But what is valuable about the ritual, however terrifying it might appear to the uninitiated, is that it is one of the few times when a wine is forced to speak for itself, rather than rely on the frippery that so often props up a dull, absurdly overpriced wine. The wine in question is no longer a fancy name on a wine list—with all the oenological

Here's an idea for you... **Blind tasting can become part of your life. Whenever anyone offers you a glass of wine, ask them not to reveal its identity until you have had a good chance to study it.**

baggage that a name entails—but simply a liquid made from the fermented juice of grapes.

BLIND TASTING

The practice of tasting wines from unmarked bottles is known in the wine trade as "blind tasting," a term that shouldn't be confused with "blind drunk"—although the former can lead to the latter. It isn't just a fun game. Every year wine experts from all over the world gather for blind tastings with the aim of awarding medals to the favored few. But blind tasting shouldn't just be the preserve of seasoned professionals. It also offers the fledgling wine taster the first step toward the nirvana of free-thinking drinking.

UNDERSTANDING OENOLOGICAL BAGGAGE

Blind tasting is an essential tool for ridding yourself of preconceptions based on the following:

- **Price.** When we dig deeply into our pockets to buy a bottle of wine, we tend to be better disposed toward its contents—not least to justify our investment.
- **Origin.** It may now be possible to make top-class wines in Uruguay, but most of us are still wedded to the idea that the world's finest wines come from the hallowed turf of areas such as Bordeaux, Burgundy, and Champagne.
- **The image projected by a label.** It's almost impossible not to be swayed by a well-designed label. Bottles with handwritten labels that have been rushed by producers to professional tastings look homemade—or, in some cases, like urine samples.

THE ROUTE TO VINOUS ENLIGHTENMENT

The only way to overcome the problem of such oenological baggage is to start to taste wine blind. My suggestion is not that you *always* taste in this way but simply that you use blind tasting to give you a grounding in the tastes and flavors displayed by the wines you are studying.

There's no great science to blind tasting. Some wine buffs wrap bottles in foil or plastic bags; others stick labels to the underside of glasses. Make sure you have plenty of glasses—if you're tasting with a friend you'll need around twenty plus tumblers for water. It's useful also to have crackers ready to purge your palate occasionally. As you taste make notes under three headings: color, aroma, and flavor. Only when you've fully understood a wine should you reveal its identity.

The secret of any tasting—and blind tasting in particular—is to get as much from a wine as you can. There's more on this subject in IDEA 5, *Put your palate through its paces.*

Try another idea...

"Blind tasting is a perpetual source of entertainment and frustration. Beginners should remember that everyone—regardless of experience or knowledge—can be fooled. But correctly identifying a wine is not as important as evaluating it even-handedly. And mistakes are more productive than successes."
DANIEL SOGG, *Wine Spectator*

Defining idea...

FINDING YOUR BEARINGS

A random selection of half a dozen red or white wines—not necessarily both colors at the same time—will give you an idea of the huge diversity of flavors and aromas displayed by wine. A selection of reds might include red Bordeaux, Rhône red, red

Burgundy, Australian Shiraz, New Zealand Pinot Noir, and Chilean Cabernet. A selection of whites might include white Loire, German Riesling, Australian Chardonnay, white Burgundy, and New Zealand Sauvignon Blanc.

COMPARE AND CONTRAST

Start making specific comparisons between pairs of wines (without revealing their identities):

- red Bordeaux + Chilean Cabernet
- red Bordeaux + red Burgundy
- red Burgundy + New Zealand Pinot Noir
- Australian Shiraz + Rhône red
- white Loire + white Burgundy
- white Loire + New Zealand Sauvignon Blanc
- Australian Chardonnay + white Burgundy
- German Riesling + Australian Chardonnay

At first the differences between one and the other will be hard to spot. Keep on coming back to the glasses and soon the distinctions will become clear. The fruity flavors of some wines may become apparent, while others may seem more acidic. You might notice that some have a nutty smell, while others are more leafy. Whatever observations you make, it is important that they are your own.

Q **Some of the flavors and aromas of the wines just seemed to merge into one. What can I do about this?**

How did it go?

A *If you aren't used to tasting a lot of different wines, their flavors can become a blur. Simply take your time and be prepared to come back to wines again and again and again. There are a few tricks that will help, such as rinsing your mouth out with water and eating a cracker between wines.*

Q **I was staggered by how some of the more expensive wines seemed quite disappointing in the context of a blind tasting. Why aren't wines served blind more often?**

A *They are. Many Mediterranean restaurants will serve wine in unmarked carafes. These wines vary in quality, but in better restaurants they are quite palatable. Drinking wine in this way can be a peculiarly liberating experience.*

4

Sweet dreams

Detecting sweetness in a wine shouldn't dampen your ardor—particularly when it's balanced with a good dose of mouthwatering acidity.

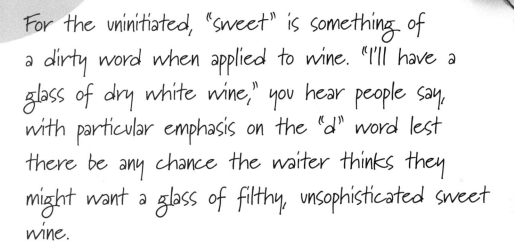

For the uninitiated, "sweet" is something of a dirty word when applied to wine. "I'll have a glass of dry white wine," you hear people say, with particular emphasis on the "d" word lest there be any chance the waiter thinks they might want a glass of filthy, unsophisticated sweet wine.

The suspicion with which many of us regard sweet wines may lie in some bad experience, deeply inscribed in our psyches, of disgustingly sugary Sherries and other fortified wines that offer nothing more than a cloying attack on the palate.

The other problem is the context in which sweet wines are traditionally drunk. Often they are served with dessert or rich cheese at the end of a meal—a fact that can make them seem far more indulgent than many other types of wine. Yet this impression is mainly the result of association rather than any innate sweetness in the wines.

Here's an idea for you... **Delicate sweetness and temperature have a symbiotic relationship. Pour half a bottle of sweetish German wine or Sauternes that is at room temperature into a decanter and put the remaining bottle in the fridge until it is lightly chilled. Next, compare the two. How does the temperature influence the flavor?**

If you're a free-thinking drinker none of these prejudices and problems will bother you. Instead, you will open your mind to the fact that while some sweet wines can be disgusting, others can be sublime. You should also be aware that a slight hint of sweetness is an essential ingredient of some of the world's most successful wines and also that some of the world's most legendary, expensive wines are really quite sweet.

SWEET AND SOUR

If you need any proof that sweetness should not be a byword for lack of sophistication in a wine you need only explore the wines of Sauternes and Chateau d'Yquem. Made from grapes that have started to rot on the vines ("botrytised," if you must know the jargon), Yquem has a near mythic reputation that means that older vintages can demand stratospheric prices at auction. Its success relies on exactly the balance that explains the success of all great sweet wines: it has sufficient acidity not to seem cloying and enough sweetness not to seem sour. This sounds simple but it's a surprisingly elusive quality.

Defining idea... *"Sweetness belongs in Mosel wines like bubbles belong in Champagne."*
NICK WEISS, Weingut St. Urbanhoff

There's a touch of irony, too, in the fact that many of the wines that wine drinkers regard as dry are, in fact, quite sweet. Much of the reason for the success of New World wines in the last decade is that they have a hint of tropical fruitiness that makes them far more approachable than the drier European wines they have eclipsed, such as Italian whites and French reds. This distinction should be clear in the following simple taste test.

TASTE TEST

- White Rioja + cheap Champagne + inexpensive Australian Chardonnay + sweetish German Riesling
- Red Burgundy + inexpensive Australian Cabernet + good quality tawny Port + inexpensive Port

HOW WAS IT FOR YOU?

Having four wines in each lineup will give a simple picture of the varying degrees of dryness and sweetness that can be found in wine. This is one of the most important factors governing which foods a wine will go with.

However, dryness or sweetness is not necessarily an indication of a wine's quality. What is key is the way either of these qualities is balanced with acidity. Any objective analysis of a wine should attempt to gauge the success of this balance. The presence of one without the other—or simply an imbalance between the two—can spell disaster.

Sweetness and acidity are two of the most important elements in determining a wine's suitability to go with food. You'll find more on the subject in IDEA 24, *Spanish highs.*

Try another idea...

"It is an almost invariable rule that anywhere hot enough to provide good fortified wine is too hot to provide the ideal climate for its consumption."
THE OXFORD COMPANION TO WINE

Defining idea...

17

WHAT'S IN A NAME?

Sweetness probably causes more confusion than any other factor. This is largely because it comes in so many styles and is created in so many ways. The Germans have Auslese, Beerenauslese, and Trockenbeerenauslese. The French have Banyuls, Barsac, and Bonnezeaux. The Italians have Reciota, Vin Santo, and Moscato. As a free-thinking drinker, you'll know that initially a good weeding out is the only solution.

How did it go?

Q   Why are drier styles of wine such as Fino Sherry, Champagne, and Sauvignon Blanc often a good choice as aperitifs?

A   *Because they are able to stimulate the appetite without desensitizing the taste buds. Try drinking a glass of cheap Port before a meal and you'll get the idea.*

Q   A couple of the whites were unbearably dry—the sort that can give you heartburn. Do they have any redeeming features?

A   *This is one of the great problems with some cheap whites—especially Champagne. However, before you dismiss a white wine as too dry, try drinking it with fish or seafood—sometimes acidity is just the thing you need.*

Q   Why is it that wines from warm countries such as Australia tend to be slightly sweeter than those from cold countries such as Germany?

A   *The warmer the weather, the riper the fruit. The riper the fruit, the sweeter the wine.*

5

Put your palate through its paces

Understanding a wine's flavor is a much more complex art than you might imagine. But rest assured, with plenty of time, practice makes perfect.

Although smelling a wine seems like a straightforward action (no more difficult than smelling a flower or a glass of milk, really), tasting it is more tricky, because different areas of the palate appear to respond in different ways to different types of flavor.

For this reason, the basic principle of tasting is to swill the wine around in your mouth like mouthwash to get as much of the wine in contact with as many of your taste buds as possible. Often it can help to aerate the wine by slurping a little air into your mouth through pursed lips. This can require practice. (If you get it wrong there's a danger that you'll splutter a mouthful of wine down the front of your shirt.)

Here's an idea for you...

To find out how your senses of taste and smell are inextricably linked it isn't necessary to delve into the anatomy of the mouth, tongue, and olfactory system. Simply try the following test: Taste a glass of wine that normally bursts with flavor and aroma while at the same time holding your nose. What more evidence do you need?

ASSESSING FLAVOR

The basic aim of tasting is to try to judge the wine's acidity, sweetness, how well the sweetness and acidity are balanced, bitterness, and how long any of these qualities stay in the mouth (known by wine buffs as their "length").

THE TOOLS

You will need: suitable glasses, still mineral water, paper labels (if blind tasting), crackers (if you are spitting), a large receptacle such as a Champagne bucket, a notebook, and a pen.

THE PROCEDURE

Everybody develops their own technique, so experiment until you find a tasting style that you feel happy with. But you might begin by using the following procedure:

1. Hold the glass up to a window (professional tasting rooms always have a good source of natural light for this purpose) and note the color. Is it dense, pale, or somewhere in between? You might also want to judge the wine's viscosity, i.e., whether it leaves a transparent coating on the sides of the glass.
2. Next, swirl the wine around in your glass (this helps to release its aroma) and then lower your nose into the glass, taking a deep breath that will gather the full effect of the wine's aroma. Don't even think about moving to the next stage until you have fully explored the scent—or lack of it—provided by the wine.

3. Now sip a small amount of wine, running it all over your palate, sucking a little air in after it.
4. Either swallow or spit—a procedure that can take years to perfect (the ideal is a fine stream of liquid so precisely aimed that you could take out a fly at fifty paces).
5. Between wines it can sometimes be useful to clean the palate with water and/or a cracker. You don't need to do this every time you try a new wine—just when you feel that you need to.

In order to maximize the flavor and aroma of the wine you are tasting, it is essential that you have the right type of glass. There's more on this in IDEA 7, *Glass act*.

Try another idea...

"If one can taste food, one can taste wine."
MICHAEL BROADBENT

Defining idea...

TAKING NOTES

There are plenty of reasons for taking notes, including the fact that they provide a record of wines that you have liked should you wish to experience them again. More important is the fact that note-taking forces you to focus on what you are tasting and to try to articulate your thoughts.

TO SPIT OR TO SWALLOW?

If you are of drinking age, you won't need any advice on this. Some people feel that they haven't really tasted a wine until they have swallowed—although there are no taste buds in the throat, so technically it isn't necessary. Others find that even a hint of alcohol can

"I am tempted to believe that smell and taste are, in fact, but a single composite sense, whose laboratory is the mouth and its chimney the nose."
BRILLAT SAVARIN

Defining idea...

21

dampen their objectivity. One option is to spit when you are making an in-depth analysis and later in the evening to swallow. With time you will soon find your ideal method.

Q   Are you suggesting that whenever I drink wine I should follow this tasting procedure?

A   *No, no, nooooooooo! You'd become a very embarrassing—not to say messy—dinner companion. However, there are means of surreptitiously sniffing, swilling, and spitting that will allow you to get the most from a wine without making a song and dance about it.*

Q   Why is assessing the color of a wine before tasting it so important?

A   *I won't bore you with the details, but simply assure you that the more you study the color of a wine, the greater will be your understanding of that wine. Before long, you'll be able to see connections between varying depths of color and the origin, flavor, and age of the wine.*

Q   Why is it that some wines—often those that are quite sweet—leave a syrupy residue on the sides of the glass?

A   *The amount of alcohol in a wine affects its viscosity. Like the color, the viscosity will prove—after extensive tasting—another pointer to the wine's flavor.*

6

Scents and sensibilities

A decent glass of wine should offer your olfactory system the most enjoyable aromatherapy treatments your palate has ever had.

But getting the most out of the fabulous aromas that good wine can offer is partly due to whether you are prepared to put your nose to work.

There are two secret signs that wine buffs employ to identify one another. One is the way that they hold a glass. *No* self-respecting wine buff holds a glass of white wine by anything other than its stem. Yes, it looks a little affected, but the reason is wholly practical—so that the clammy embrace of a sweaty palm won't raise the temperature of the contents.

The other sign is the way that wine buffs taste wines poured for their approval in restaurants. People who are not wine buffs tend to take a hurried sip before nodding appreciatively. Wine buffs, on the other hand, leave the glass on the table and gently rotate the glass while holding the base of the stem between their fingers. After a few seconds they lift the glass to their nose and take a deep,

Here's an idea for you... **Too often it is possible to sip the contents of a glass without pausing to appreciate the wine's most important feature—its smell. Try to get into the habit of never tasting a wine until you have fully explored its aroma. Make sure that you smell the wine and return to it three or four times before eventually letting it enter your mouth. This simple ritual will do a huge amount to accelerate your understanding of wine.**

prolonged sniff. Not a molecule of liquid passes their lips. Ostensibly, the philosophy underlying this approach is that it is possible to judge whether a wine has been corked purely on the basis of its smell. But the procedure also suggests that the wine buff has graduated to the level where their enjoyment of wine is based as much on its aroma as its flavor. And this should be one of the aims of anyone who wants to maximize the pleasure that wine has to offer. The reason that wine offers such an enduring fascination is that it is one of the few liquids that can express such a complex range of aromas.

SMELL FIRST, TASTE LATER

A surprising number of people rarely smell the wine they are drinking, with the result that they miss out on 80 percent of its pleasure—particularly when drinking wine with fabulously aromatic qualities. The simple rule is never, ever to taste a wine without smelling it first. Only then will you begin to appreciate the wonderful array of aromas that wine can provide.

Beware of lists of grape varieties and their attributes. A free-thinking drinker should develop the confidence to develop their *own* opinions about wine. If you're told that the typical aroma of Transylvanian Pinot Noir is "sawdust from a hamster's cage," there's a danger that "sawdust from a hamster's cage" is how you will perceive this aroma for evermore, even if a better analogy is "dust from old floorboards." Because wine is such a wildly subjective field, it is essential that you build up your own descriptive vocabulary. One taster's "deliciously tropical fruit character" is another's "smells horribly like 7-Up."

Instead of providing such a list, I'm going to suggest another tasting menu that will help you come to grips with the huge range of aromas offered by wine.

TASTING MENU

When exploring the wines listed below, write down the names of other smells that they remind you of. Not all these wines have been chosen for their distinctive aroma—some are included simply to demonstrate the range of characters wine can offer.

Aromatic whites: New Zealand Sauvignon, Gewurztraminer, German Riesling, Australian Chardonnay.

Scented reds: Good-quality red Bordeaux, New Zealand Pinot Noir, good-quality Australian Shiraz, Australian Cabernet.

Try another idea...

Once you have learned to appreciate the attractive smells offered by wine, you will also learn to recognize the bad ones. After trying the taste test in this chapter you might want to turn to IDEA 19, *Cork talk*, to consider one of the most unwelcome smells—cork. In order to fully appreciate the smell of a wine it is important to have the right glass. There's more on this in IDEA 7, *Glass act*.

Defining idea...

"Smell is the most important part of wine tasting. You can only perceive four tastes— sweet, sour, bitter, and salt— but the average person can smell over 2,000 different scents, and each wine has over 200 of its own."
KEVIN ZRALY, *Windows on the World Complete Wine Course*

COMPARE AND CONTRAST

Having lined up your anonymous glasses of wine, allow yourself plenty of time to fully appreciate their aromas—and don't even think of tasting them until you have thoroughly explored their characters. Remember, the aromas of individual wines are defined by how they compare with one another.

How did it go?

Q   I am worried that if I sniff too enthusiastically there's a chance that wine will go up my nose. How do I avoid this?

A   *You don't need to inhale the wine. Simply make sure that it isn't slopping around in the glass when you smell it.*

Q   Why do some wines—particularly whites—seem more aromatic than others?

A   *Much depends on the climate in which the grapes were grown. Wines from cool areas such as Germany and New Zealand tend to be more fragrant than those from hot areas.*

Q   Are there some wines that have little aroma?

A   *Yes, there are a few neutral styles of white, particularly from Italy. Lack of aroma isn't necessarily a sign that a wine is no good. Some people like neutral wines because they don't compete with the flavors of food.*

7

Glass act

In order to fully appreciate the smell of a wine it is essential that you have the right glass. But don't allow yourself to be confused—or conned—by anyone who tries to sell you a different glass for every conceivable type of wine.

The perfect wineglass is much simpler—and cheaper—than you might be led to believe.

The more wines you try, the more you'll discover that their tastes and smells can be heavily influenced by factors such as their temperature, the food that you're eating with them, and whether you have just brushed your teeth or eaten some chili.

Another factor is the shape of the glass. In the world of wine buffery there are two schools of thought on the subject: a relaxed approach and an obsessive approach (sitting on the fence is not an option). One of the rules of wine buffery is that it is always important to have an opinion on *everything*. But such opinions ought to be *yours* rather than anyone else's.

TWO KINDS OF GLASSES

In order to come to grips with the theory, you need to do some homework—for which you will need two glasses.

Here's an idea for you... **Try the taste test with other types of wine. How do the flavor and aroma of a good Fino Sherry compare when they are tasted in an old-fashioned thimble-sized Sherry glass, a tulip-shaped copita, and a large wineglass? How does red Bordeaux vary when it is tasted in a tumbler and in a high-quality wineglass? Only extensive tasting will help you understand the complex relationship between a wine and the glass you drink it in.**

The first glass should be the ubiquitous Paris goblet, the glass that has a modestly sized spherical bowl on a stem and is beloved by pubs and seaside boardinghouses because it is both cheap and capable of withstanding almost anything that a dishwasher can throw at it.

The second glass will require more investment. It must be larger and tulip-shaped, i.e., the circumference of the rim should be smaller than that of the bowl, and the glass must be thinner than the type used to make an everyday drinking glass. The test of good-quality glass is that it resonates when you flick it with your fingernail.

TASTE TEST

Pour about 4 ounces of an aromatic white wine such as a high-quality New Zealand Sauvignon Blanc into each glass. In the smaller glass you will notice that the surface of the wine is much closer to the rim than in the larger glass, where it occupies a relatively small proportion of the bowl. This fact will become more strongly evident when you go to smell the wine: Your nose will be much closer to the wine in the smaller glass than in the larger glass.

QUESTIONS TO ASK YOURSELF

1. A question of smell. How does the smell of the wine in the smaller glass compare with the smell of the wine in the larger glass?
2. A question of taste. Is there any difference between the flavor of the wine in the small glass and flavor of the wine in the large glass?

EXAMINING YOUR FINDINGS

There is no real science to choosing the right glass. The most important factor is simply that one's appreciation of the smell and flavor of a wine is influenced by the shape of the glass and the thickness of its rim. A large, tulip-shaped glass captures the aroma and if not overfilled will provide sufficient space for the aroma of the wine to express itself. Combined with a thin rim—which is less intrusive in the tasting experience than a thick rim—it offers the ideal vessel in which to taste wine. Another obvious advantage of drinking wine from a tulip-shaped glass is that it allows you to swill the wine around in the glass without it spilling over the edges.

Choosing the right wineglass will help you to maximize your enjoyment of a wine's aromas, a subject explored in IDEA 6, *Scents and sensibilities*.

Try another idea...

"Burgundy, particularly red Burgundy, has come to be served in glass balloons, so large that they resemble goldfish bowls. The idea, apart from lusty exhibitionism, is that a good Burgundy can offer such a rich panoply of aromas that they should be given every chance to escape the wine and titillate the taster. Most wine connoisseurs use the shape on a reduced scale."
THE OXFORD COMPANION TO WINE

Defining idea...

LEARNING TO TELL FACT FROM FICTION

There are those who believe that in order to maximize your enjoyment of a wine you have to drink from a glass that has been tailored to bring out that wine's best features. The only way to test the theory is to invest the considerable sum required to equip yourself with a huge array of specialist glasses and then let your nose and palate judge for themselves. Alternatively, you could save yourself a fortune and satisfy yourself with two or three glass shapes.

How did it go?

Q   Is there a reason that Sherry is traditionally served in small glasses?

A   *No reason at all—except possible post-war austerity. There's no reason why Sherry shouldn't be served in an ordinary wineglass.*

Q   Are there any wines that are not suited to Paris goblets?

A   *No.*

Q   Why is it that bad wine sometimes tastes better in tumblers than in tulip-shaped glasses?

A   *Bad wine rarely smells great, so by tasting it in an open glass rather than an enclosed one you are allowing the unattractive aromas to disperse.*

8
Understanding Chardonnay

The Chardonnay grape produces far more than just one wine. Depending on where it is grown and how it is handled, it will produce a vast array of styles—some dull, some delicious.

Chardonnay is now so ubiquitous that for some people it has become something of a joke. Yet the grapes come in such great diversity that it is hard to generalize about them.

So when people say that they have "Chardonnay fatigue" or that they are members of the ABC ("anything but Chardonnay") movement, which particular kind of Chardonnay are they referring to? Chablis, Meursault, or Macon? Southern French, northern Italian, or Sicilian? Or is it Australian Chardonnay that they are disillusioned with? And, if so, is it Aussie Chardonnay from the Hunter, the Yarra, or the Margaret River? Is it oaky Chardonnay or unoaked Chardonnay? The list of variations is almost infinite and, though there are some common characteristics, these are massively outnumbered by the shades of difference that occur in this extraordinarily adaptable grape variety. Depending on where it is grown, Chardonnay can demonstrate a huge variety of traits, from a steely, minerally austerity to an oaky, nutty richness.

Here's an idea for you...

Remember that when you are tasting the wines on the tasting menu you are doing so without food—or perhaps nothing more enticing than a dry cracker. If possible, crank up your tasting session by trying the wines with food. Examine how the different styles combine with the flavors of spicy food, fish, and red meat.

Like any grape it can also make wines that are extremely bland—and it is because of these that many better-quality examples have been given a bad name. But the reason for the grape's commercial success must also be that even when Chardonnay isn't well made it can still be much better than the basic examples of other white wines, such as Riesling or Sauvignon Blanc. It is perhaps this fact that has encouraged winemakers all over the world to make it their number one grape.

A QUICK HISTORY OF CHARDONNAY

In the beginning there was Chablis, the most popular of all white Burgundies, the wine that college students drank with a roast on a Sunday (if they weren't drinking red Bordeaux). Then the Australians wanted a piece of the action and during the '60s and '70s Chardonnay became increasingly popular, particularly in areas such as the Hunter Valley, which is now regarded as the spiritual home of Aussie Chardonnay. The Californians planted it, too, and during the '80s and '90s it rapidly appeared in wine regions from Chile to South Africa. The rest is history. Chardonnay is now one of the most successful, widely recognized grape varieties, which winemakers love for its adaptability and drinkers for its approachability.

TASTE TEST

As with any grape variety the only way to find your way around all the different styles is to put your nose and palate to work. A good introduction should include expensive Chablis, expensive Californian Chardonnay, inexpensive oaky Australian Chardonnay, unoaked Australian Chardonnay, and Hungarian Chardonnay.

COMPARE AND CONTRAST

There were doubtless times in this taste test when you wondered whether you were tasting the same grape. Chardonnnay grown in the relatively chilly climes of Burgundy will inevitably have a very different character from one grown in the sunny climes of New South Wales. But it isn't just the weather that affects the flavor of a wine. So, too, does the way that it is made. Ask yourself some of the following questions. Were some of the wines sweeter or drier than others? Stronger and more robust? A little more acidic? Slightly creamier? Fruitier?

Do you think that the flavor of any of the wines that you tasted might have been influenced by the climate in the region where they were made? For more on this subject turn to IDEA 13, *Come rain or shine*, and IDEA 17, *The reign of terroir*.

Try another idea...

"The wine critics might pine for something else to write about, and the wine experts may decide that they want to explore the flavors available from other grape varieties, but for the vast majority of wine drinkers the Chardonnay revolution has only just begun, and to many people good dry white simply equals Chardonnay."
OZ CLARKE

Defining idea...

How did
it go?

Q **Until I read this book, I didn't realize that white Burgundies such as Chablis and Meursault are made out of Chardonnay. Is there a reason that the name of the grape doesn't appear on the label?**

A *Yes. Historically the French don't put the names of grape varieties on their bottles, largely because they think that a wine's origin is more important than its ingredient. As you might have discovered through comparing the Chardonnays listed above, this idea isn't purely French eccentricity. Knowing the origin of a wine will sometimes offer more clues about how it will taste than will knowing which grape it was made from.*

Q **When I revealed the identity of the wines, I was surprised by how little correlation there was between price and enjoyment, particularly in the case of the Chablis. Am I missing something?**

A *No, you're not alone. One wine writer recently compared Burgundian Chardonnay to battery acid. The problem is that tastes change. Now that people have discovered the joys of softer, more approachable styles of Chardonnay from the southern hemisphere, white wines from Burgundy can sometimes feel a little thin and mean in comparison.*

Q **Some of the Chardonnays tasted thin and watery and had very little flavor. Why is that?**

A *This isn't the fault of the grapes, but arises from factors such as the climate of the area where it was grown and whether the vines were irrigated. With the exception of white Burgundy, you will pretty much get what you pay for. But if you aren't a great fan of oak you might find some of the more expensive wines from California and Australia a little overbearing.*

9

Whites with attitude

The more obscure the grape, the more exciting the range of flavors. Learn to love the exotic pleasures of offbeat white grapes.

The world would be a very dull place if we all just drank Chardonnay and Sauvignon Blanc. However approachable these wines might be, there are times when you'll want to treat yourself to a wider range of flavors and aromas.

There are plenty of more obscure whites worth trying—some of them toe-curlingly unfashionable but nevertheless extraordinarily delicious.

UNFASHIONABLE GRAPE NUMBER 1: RIESLING

German Riesling once ruled the world. Fresh and often light in style, it was perfect for drinking at lunchtime. But in the '80s the arrival of sunnier wines from the southern hemisphere meant the end of the road for Riesling's popularity. However, plenty of delicious examples still abound, both from Germany and increasingly from other cool climate regions such as New Zealand.

Here's an idea for you...

Set yourself the following challenge. For a month drink only white wines other than Chardonnay and Sauvignon Blanc. Whenever you're faced with a row of bottles in a wine shop—or a list of wines in a restaurant—opt for anything you haven't tried before. The more you taste around, the more happy discoveries you'll make.

UNFASHIONABLE GRAPE NUMBER 2: GEWÜRZTRAMINER

A sublimely scented wine whose spiritual home is in Alsace. Gewürztraminer has always suffered from the fact that it is difficult not only to spell but also to say.

UNFASHIONABLE GRAPE NUMBER 3: PINOT GRIGIO/GRIS

The thin whites of northern Italy (known as Pinot Grigio) have done much to ruin the reputation of a grape that in the right hands can produce rich scented wines that make ideal partners to Asian food.

INCREASINGLY FASHIONABLE GRAPE NUMBER 1: SEMILLON

The classic white grape of Bordeaux is now grown all over the world, notably in Australia, where it produces whites that put their French ancestors to shame.

INCREASINGLY FASHIONABLE GRAPE NUMBER 2: VIOGNIER

In the Rhône Valley, Viognier makes wines with an almost mythical reputation—and breathtaking price tags. In the South of France and Australia it provides easy-drinking wines that make a good alternative to Chardonnay.

INCREASINGLY FASHIONABLE GRAPE NUMBER 3: VERDELHO

Once popular in Madeira, this obscure grape variety is now being used to make distinctive wines in Australia, particularly in the Hunter Valley in New South Wales.

TASTE TEST

- Australian Verdelho
- Southern French Viognier
- Australian Semillon
- New Zealand Pinot Gris
- Alsace Gewürztraminer
- Dry Riesling
- Chardonnay
- Sauvignon Blanc

One of the characters that you might have encountered when trying these wines is sweetness. If you were flummoxed by this quality you'll find more discussion of the subject in IDEA 4, *Sweet dreams.*

Try another idea...

"The discovery of a wine is a greater moment than the discovery of a constellation. The universe is too full of stars."
BENJAMIN FRANKLIN

Defining idea...

You don't have to try all these wines at once. Four or five will suffice. The Chardonnay and Sauvignon have been included on the list so you have some familiar flavors and aromas to compare the more offbeat wines against. In each case consider the aroma, flavor, color, how it might go with food (some experimentation would be good), and whether it would make a good aperitif.

THE JOY OF DIVERSITY

The purpose of broadening your vinous horizons by trying a wide array of weird and wonderful whites is not just to develop universal tastes. The greater number of flavors and aromas you're aware of, the greater chance you'll have of finding wines that serve a specific purpose, such as offering a good match with food. Chardonnay and Sauvignon might make good bedfellows for a wide variety of everyday dishes, but are they really the right choice for a Thai green curry, a delicately flavored sorbet, or a fragrant pasta dish?

THE JOY OF A CLANKING FRIDGE

In addition to conducting a taste test, it helps to have a few bottles of wine on hand at the same time. Even without the help of a preserving system, wine stored in a stoppered bottle will stay in good condition for two to three days. When exploring offbeat whites keep a handful in the fridge so that you can dip into them as you try different dishes. You'll be amazed what discoveries you make. The same goes for red wines: The more bottles you have open at any one time, the more opportunities you'll have to compare them with different types of food—and with one another.

Q Frankly, I found some of the wines you suggested I try rather disappointing. What do you say to that?

How did it go?

A *That's fine. Some of them might not have been particularly good examples. Or you may have experienced flavors that you're not used to detecting in a white wine, such as sweetness, nuttiness, or even a strange whiff of gas. Don't be put off. You will eventually find a style of wine that you do like or you may come to appreciate sweetness, nuttiness, or gasiness in a wine. Remember the first time that you ever tried wine? You probably thought it was disgusting and slightly bitter. How things have changed...*

Q But if I have a favorite white wine why would I want to find an alternative?

A *Even if you never tire of the familiar flavors of your favorite Chardonnay or Sauvignon Blanc, there will be times when you either want or need a white with a different character. It might be a hot summer's evening and, although your current passion might be for a big blockbuster Californian Chardonnay, you really want something light and refreshing that maybe has a hint of sweetness and perhaps a floral aroma. Or imagine that you have painstakingly created a delicious Thai recipe with subtle, fragile flavors. Would you really want to smother them with an attention-grabbing Sauvignon? A discreet, similarly delicate-scented white might be a better choice. Try it out.*

10

Grape expectations

Mastering the art of telling one grape from another is the easy part. But, such is the intervention that goes on during the winemaking process, the *really* tough question is whether grapes truly matter.

There is no great secret to grape spotting. The more that blind tasting focuses your palate, the more the characteristic traits of each grape will shine through. Slowly but surely one grape will become as distinct from another as night is from day.

The more familiar that you become with a grape, the more you will spot subtle imprints left on it by various factors, especially the weather. For example, Chardonnay grapes grown in the sweltering heat of southeast Australia will produce wines with flavors that differ hugely from those grown in the chillier climes of Burgundy.

Here's an idea for you...

Try to familiarize yourself with the major grape varieties by always trying to guess which ones are in the wine you are drinking. Initially you'll often get them wrong, but the more you focus on this skill, the more you'll find your way.

But it isn't just the weather that will affect the flavor of a wine, but also the way the wine is made. It might have been given a nutty, smoky flavor by being kept in oak barrels or by having a giant bag of oak chips suspended in it, or it might have been mixed with some other grape. Winemaking has become such an exact science that it is possible to manipulate the flavor of a grape in almost any direction that the winemaker wishes to take it. In many cases this has led to an increasingly homogeneous style as winemakers create wines that are intended to appeal to as many people as possible.

TASTE TEST

To demonstrate the diverse flavors that can be displayed by one grape variety, try a taste test. Comparison of an Australian Chardonnay and a white Burgundy is a good example: the character and aroma of the wines are likely to be so different that to the untrained palate and nose they might as well be completely different grapes. To explore the subject further, try any of the following combinations:

- Burgundian Chardonnay + Australian Chardonnay
- Burgundian Pinot Noir + New Zealand Pinot Noir
- Loire Sauvignon Blanc + Chilean Sauvignon Blanc
- sweet German Riesling + Australian dry Riesling

COMPARE AND CONTRAST

In most cases you will probably have found very different personalities demonstrated by the same grape and you might well be asking a question that is almost heretical in the brave new world of wine appreciation: How important are grapes?

The subject of how wines made with just one grape compare with those made with two or more is discussed in greater detail in IDEA 18, *In the mix*.

Try another idea...

THE VIEW FROM FRANCE

Until recently, few French wine lovers gave a fig about grapes—and many of them still don't. To traditionalists, the origin of a wine is far, far more important than its ingredients—a belief that has much to do with the idea that wine is the product of soil and weather rather than grapes and winemaking. This is the reason that until a few years ago the name of a grape variety was a rare sight on a bottle of French wine. Instead, most still use the name of its place of origin, such as Bordeaux, Champagne, or Rhône.

Many French winemakers would also argue that because some of their wines are made from a blend of three or four grapes the finished product is more important than the ingredients. Some Bordeaux reds, for example, include two or three grape varieties and some from the South of France include more.

"If oenologists can rightly take the credit for much of the improvement in the overall standard of winemaking, they are also accountable for some of the decrease in character and individuality of fine wines in certain classic areas."
MICHAEL BROADBENT

Defining idea...

43

THE VIEW FROM THE NEW WORLD

A winemaker in Australia, New Zealand, Chile, or South Africa would beg to differ. For them, wine should be a shining example of the grape it was made from. Chardonnay should conform to the classic fruit and oak combination. Sauvignon Blanc should be fresh and zingy. Cabernet should be deep and berryish. Merlot should be soft and velvety. This, they believe, not only focuses the attention of the winemaker but also simplifies matters by offering the market recognizable names with a range of flavors and aromas that are easy to identify.

TAKE YOUR PICK

Although these two views appear to be contradictory, they aren't necessarily mutually exclusive. There are some wines that express the place where they were made and others that express the grape they were made from. Even if this statement sounds like an excuse for sitting on the fence, it is probably the best option in an area as subjective as wine, where there are few truly black and white rules.

Q   **I was astonished by how the same grape can create such a huge range of flavors and aromas. If grapes can produce such diverse styles why do we need to worry about which grapes wines are made from?**

How did it go?

A   *Imagine that the grape is like a brand of car and all the variations such as country and style (oaked and unoaked) are different models. The former gives you a general idea of what the wine or car might be like, the latter a more specific picture.*

Q   **The most fickle grape seemed to be Riesling. Is it supposed to be a sweet wine or a dry wine?**

A   *Riesling, like many grapes, can be used to make wines with a variety of levels of sweetness. What is unusual about Riesling is that it makes not just great dry wines but also sublime sweet ones.*

Q   **Isn't the approach of New World winemakers rather simplistic?**

A   *Not really. There is an argument that wines that are made from just one grape variety have helped consumers to understand wine better. Besides, some very sophisticated wines—white and red Burgundy, for example—are made from just one grape variety.*

11

What winemakers do

If only wine consisted of nothing more than the fermented juice of grapes! In fact, there's a great deal of intervention in the winery, some good, some rather distasteful.

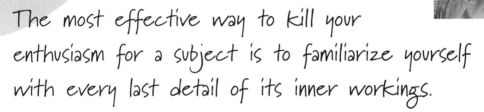

The most effective way to kill your enthusiasm for a subject is to familiarize yourself with every last detail of its inner workings.

Fortunately, there are only a few aspects of wine production that you must know about—those that directly influence the wine's flavor, which is why you won't find much discussion here of processes such as fining, filtering, and racking. Much of what happens to grapes, particularly those used to make cheap wines, involves compensating for poor-quality grapes. If all grapes were grown in ideal conditions, there would be little need to do much more than crush them and then ferment the juice that remains. For very expensive wines, that is more or less what happens: little is subtracted, other than skins, and little is added.

For mass-produced wines, the reality is rather different. In order to maximize the quantity of grapes produced by vines, quality falls by the wayside—with the result that people in white coats are required to do their best to compensate. In some parts of the world these efforts can take all sorts of forms, from the addition of everything from chemicals such as tartaric, citric, and malic acid to giant perforated bags of oak shavings that mimic the far more expensive business of aging the wine

Here's an idea for you...

If you really want to understand the difference between wines that are made with painstaking care and those that are made in industrial conditions, simply taste them side by side. Try comparing the most basic Australian Shiraz with an expensive Syrah from the Rhône Valley and the flavors will talk far more elegantly than any technical guide to winemaking.

in oak barrels. Gleaming, state-of-the-art temperature-controlled equipment helps, too, as does the practice of blending grapes of different varieties or grown in different areas in order to iron out imperfections. The leaps and bounds in technology mean that winemakers are now capable of making silk purses out of sows' ears, so that cheap wine tastes better now than ever before.

TASTE TEST

Tasting wine won't help you learn much about the winemaking process but it will give you an insight into the effect that it has. Try tasting some grape juice, very oaky Chardonnay, and an unoaked Australian Chardonnay.

COMPARE AND CONTRAST

Grape juice is wine that hasn't been fermented, aged in oak, or generally messed around with, so it provides a useful comparison to gauge the impact that the winemaking process has had on the other wines. The two other wines give you an opportunity to compare wine that has and hasn't been oaked.

FATHOMLESS DEPTHS

Be aware that the depths of knowledge that can be plumbed are almost fathomless. Once you've come to grips with how wine is made, you can find out about the diverse sorts of oak used to make barrels, about vineyard management (including the mind-bending business of how the vines are trained), the amount of pruning that takes place, the question of yield. None of these subjects is static. Like any scientific subject, they are constantly evolving and if you really want to earn your colors as an armchair oenologist you have to be aware of every new development. In order to do that, you'll have to subscribe to every technical wine publication you can lay your hands on. The question to ask yourself is whether immersing yourself in all this knowledge will really help to deepen your understanding of wine—or whether, indeed, it might detract from the only two features of any wine that really matter: its flavor and aroma.

There is a chance to come to grips with the finer points of oaking in IDEA 12, *Waiter, there's some oak in my glass.*

Try another idea...

"It is not necessary to know all about the internal combustion engine in order to drive a car. It is, however, generally agreed that driving lessons are essential and, in the final analysis, practice makes perfect. In the same way a detailed knowledge of viniculture and viticulture is not a prerequisite for the enjoyment of wine. However, an understanding of basic principles, a degree of experience, and a fairly discerning palate are essential if wine is to be appreciated as something more than just an ordinary drink."
MICHAEL BROADBENT

Defining idea...

49

How did
it go?

Q **When I compared the Australian Shiraz with the expensive red Rhône they seemed as though they could have been made from two completely different grapes. However, while the Rhône was four times more expensive than the Shiraz, it wasn't really four times better. Why's that?**

A *It's because with wine there's no correlation between the amount of money spent and the enjoyment given. But then the same can also be true of all manner of consumer goods, from clothes to cars.*

Q **One of the major differences between the grape juice and the Chardonnay was the lack of alcohol in the former. How does alcohol influence the flavor of a wine?**

A *Alcohol is one of the least discussed ingredients in wine (except in the context of hangovers). The irony is that although alcohol is flavorless it has a significant impact on the character of a wine because it acts as a vehicle for other aromas, helping to transmit them to our olfactory system. On the whole, you'll find that the higher the alcohol content of a wine, the more flavor it will have.*

Q **Is all wine that is produced by an industrial process dull?**

A *There are exceptions but, on the whole, yes. However, there's nothing intrinsically wrong with dull wine. And dull is a big improvement on disgusting, which is what most cheap wines used to be.*

12

Waiter, there's some oak in my glass

Of all the flavors in wine, oak is the most easily identified. Here's a guide to spotting it—and to using such disparaging put-downs as "mouth-puckeringly oaky" with confidence.

Oakiness is one of the easiest characteristics to spot in a wine, which is undoubtedly the reason that it is one that is often seized by novice wine enthusiasts as a good talking point for their earliest oenological discourse.

But for some drinkers it might come as a surprise that oaky flavors are there in the first place. The reason is simpler than you might imagine. Before the advent of stainless steel and plastic, oak offered a convenient material with which to make barrels in which wine could be stored, aged, and transported. As well as being easy to work, durable, and watertight, oak was found to bestow a flavor that has a natural affinity with the flavor of wine. So, although the use of oak barrels is no longer essential in the winemaking process, it is considered a useful means of enhancing and manipulating the flavor of wine. And in today's high-tech

Here's an idea for you...

Whenever you taste a wine, try to determine whether it has been oaked—and, if it has, how successfully it has been done. With time you'll discover the amount of oakiness you like in a wine.

winemaking industry in which the contents of a bottle seem increasingly divorced from the vine, oak has the attraction of making wine seem less clinical.

For makers of inexpensive, mass-market wines, there is a problem in the fact that oak barrels are hugely expensive. For many winemakers, the answer is to treat their wines with what look like giant teabags full of wooden chips that impart the flavor of oak without the expense of oak barrels.

How much does it matter whether a wine derives its oakiness from oak chips or real oak barrels? Not much at all. As the free-thinking drinker that you're becoming, you will appreciate that the most important feature of any wine is not how it was made but its taste and aroma.

TASTE TEST

You'll find the flavor of oak in both red and white wines. To explore the subject it makes sense to focus on just one grape variety. Try the following wines side by side: unoaked Chardonnay; medium-priced oaky Australian, Californian, or South African Chardonnay; oaked Burgundian Chardonnay; and expensive oaked Californian Chardonnay. It is often suggested that oaky wines make good partners to food, so you might like to try these wines with a meal. Ideally, it would be useful to try them with a wide variety of dishes such as chicken, fish, and red meat.

COMPARE AND CONTRAST

Just tasting your way around these wines will quickly give you a handle on the different effects that oak can have on a wine. For most people, oak is simply a question of personal taste—like goat cheese or coffee.

Oak plays an important part in a wine's suitability as a partner to food. There's more on matching food and wine in IDEA 33, *The secret of a happy marriage.*

Try another idea...

THE BALANCING ACT

Giving a wine just the right amount of oaky flavor is one of the greatest tests of a winemaker's skills. Much of the success depends on other characteristics such as acidity and sweetness. As a rule of thumb, the better quality (and more expensive) the wine, the better the balance of all these components will be. Much also comes down to the winemaking philosophy of the winemaker. In France, for example, the emphasis is on ensuring that oakiness is so well integrated that it is almost imperceptible. In the southern hemisphere, however, winemakers prefer to give it to you straight.

OAK AND FOOD

Remember, too, that the flavor of a wine is massively influenced by whether or not you drink it with food. A wine that might taste overbearingly oaky on its own will seem completely different when it is drunk with grilled chicken. There are many foods—particularly those with very strong flavors—that will make an oaky wine seem considerably less oaky.

"The real asset of an oak barrel is physical. It allows just the right amount of interplay between oxygen, wine, and the wood's own characteristics to encourage red wine to settle gradually and acquire extra smoothness and stability."
JANCIS ROBINSON, *Confessions of a Wine Lover*

Defining idea...

OAK AND THE FREE-THINKING DRINKER

Recently, wine bores have railed against oak as though it were some illicit drug. Yes, oak can overpower a wine that might otherwise be fresh and vibrant. However, the argument is far from clear-cut. The truth is that there are good oaky wines and bad oaky wines in equal measure. But, used well, oak is to wine what seasoning is to food—and with all matters of taste it is essential to keep an open mind.

How did it go?

Q Why is it that some of the wines that were supposed to have been oaked didn't seem particularly oaky at all?

A Probably because they had been well oaked. Very well-oaked wines have a subtle nuttiness that you might not notice immediately. However, you would certainly notice the difference if it wasn't there.

Q Why is it that some of the very heavily oaked white wines I have tasted were yellower than those that were unoaked?

A This is one of the unattractive side effects of the oaking process. Sometimes the wines get yellower as they get older.

Q On the whole, I prefer the fresher flavors of unoaked wines. Are there any types of food that go well with that style of wine?

A Yes, these wines are well suited to summery dishes such as salads, seafood, and fish dishes with subtle flavors.

13

Come rain or shine

One of the reasons that wine has a huge range of different flavors and aromas is that grapes are enormously sensitive to the climate they are grown in.

In the popular imagination a caricature of a wine buff is a red-nosed elderly man who drones on about the differences between wines made in the northern and southern extremes of a valley.

The intimation is that the idea that two wines made just a few miles apart can have different sets of characteristics is absurd. But ask any gardener and they'll tell you that a distance of just a couple of feet can have a huge impact on the success of a plant. Take into account the fact that grapes have an almost unique ability to express differences and the notion doesn't seem quite so far-fetched.

This is one of the reasons that really rabid wine enthusiasts have an almost obsessive interest in geology and topography. Yet in the same way that to derive enjoyment from classical music you don't have to be intimately acquainted with details of the score, the instruments, and the orchestra, you also don't need degrees in

Here's an idea for you... **When tasting wine blind, try to guess whether it is from the northern or southern hemisphere before revealing its identity.**

meteorology and geography to enjoy wine. Free-thinking drinkers simply need to take on board a few basic ideas to help them understand how the weather affects the taste and aroma of wine.

SUNNIER MEANS JUICIER

A grape is no different from any other type of fruit. Bite into an apple in early summer when it is still small and green and it will taste wincingly sour. By autumn the same apple will have been exposed to plenty of sun and become sweet and juicy. Grapes follow exactly the same pattern; those grown in different parts of the world are exposed to greater or lesser amounts of sun and so will display very different characteristics.

Champagne is a good example of a wine made from grapes that are the product of a cool northern climate. Because the grapes are never exposed to enough sun to make them fat, ripe, and juicy, they make wines that are typically quite acidic. When the same grapes grown farther south—say in the Languedoc—are used to make wine, the wines are fruitier because they have been exposed to a greater amount of sunlight.

TASTE TEST

- Inexpensive white Burgundy + fruity Australian Chardonnay
- Inexpensive red Bordeaux + fruity Australian Cabernet

COMPARE AND CONTRAST

When comparing each of these pairs of wine, try to picture vineyards in Burgundy and Bordeaux that for many months of the year are as sodden and overcast as any region in northern Europe. Next, cast your mind several thousand miles southeast to the sun-baked earth of Australia and consider how the warmer climate might have affected the flavor of the grapes.

The influence that weather has on the flavor of wine is one of the arguments central to the French concept of terroir. You'll find more on this in IDEA 17, *The reign of terroir*.

Try another idea...

HOT VERSUS COLD

One of the reasons that wines made in countries such as Australia, Chile, and South Africa have become so popular in the last decade is that warmer temperatures produce wines that are fruitier and more approachable than those made in Europe's chillier climes. Old-school wine buffs will argue that, though the sunny vineyards of the deep south might make cheap wines with uncomplicated tropical fruit flavor, wines with such elusive qualities as "finesse" and "complexity" tend to come from the cooler vineyards of Bordeaux, Burgundy, and Alsace. Modernists, on the other hand, claim that warmer vineyards create wines that are more user-friendly than the thin, mean products of the chilly, rain-lashed north. The more you taste, the clearer it will become that the difference between the wines made in these two different climates is not one of quality—it simply concerns their character. And as an increasingly enlightened drinker you will realize that it pays to keep an open mind.

"There is no such thing as bad weather, only different kinds of good weather."
JOHN RUSKIN

Defining idea...

WHATEVER THE WEATHER

The greater extremes of weather in European winemaking regions—hailstones, devastating storms, and floods are not unknown during key parts of the growing season—make producers far more susceptible to whatever nature can throw at them. For devotees of classic wines such as Bordeaux and Burgundy, this is the price to be paid for the high quality of wines in better years. The evenhanded character of the weather in the southern hemisphere means that vintages tend to be far more consistent, which makes the obsession of old-school wine buffs with the comparison of different years largely irrelevant to the consideration of New World wines.

How did it go?

Q   Why do all the prestigious wine regions seem to be in the chilly northern hemisphere?

A   *Because there is a winemaking tradition in Northern Europe that dates back to Roman times. After the fall of the Roman Empire, the expertise remained, largely thanks to the monastic system. The result is that areas such as Bordeaux, Burgundy, and Champagne were well established long before Europeans started colonizing Australia, Chile, and South Africa.*

Q   Why is it that I find many of the wines from very hot climates rather overpowering?

A   *Because grapes grown in warmer climates become much riper, they make wines with much bolder, sometimes sweeter flavors than those made in cooler climates. It's a style that people used to subtle Burgundies, red Bordeaux, and German Riesling can find hard to adjust to.*

14

Growing old gracefully

Do all wines improve with age? If not, which wines do? Take your palate on a journey into the past.

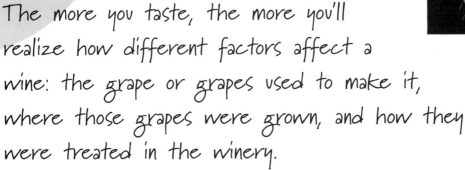

The more you taste, the more you'll realize how different factors affect a wine: the grape or grapes used to make it, where those grapes were grown, and how they were treated in the winery.

But those aren't the only factors. The flavor of many wines is intimately related to two key factors: the year it was made and how long ago it was made. These two factors are inextricably linked. When wine buffs discuss the "vintage" of a wine, they are referring to the weather conditions in the year it was made and the impact these might have had on the wine. But as the wine gets older they will also be referring to the way that it is has aged.

It sounds complicated, doesn't it? But it becomes less so when you unburden yourself of some baggage that may be lurking at the back of your mind. Let's consider two commonly held beliefs.

Here's an idea for you...

Almost everyone has old bottles of wine lurking in cupboards. Once you've established that a bottle isn't worth hundreds of dollars (the best way to check the value of a wine is to look at the websites of specialist merchants), open it. Even if it's a wine that wasn't made for aging, it will help you to understand the way that the character of a wine changes over the years.

MYTH 1: A VINTAGE YEAR ON THE BOTTLE INDICATES QUALITY

This is true of only a tiny proportion of wines, mostly European. Like so many issues relating to wine, it is another case of southern versus northern winemaking. In the northern regions, where the climate changes dramatically from one year to the next, wine is more likely to reflect the year in which it was made. In the southern regions, where the weather tends to be less temperamental, wine is more likely to be pretty much the same from year to year.

But even in Europe vintage variation is becoming less of an issue than it once was. The leaps and bounds in winemaking technology have enabled producers to iron out the effects that a poor harvest might have on a wine. The truth is that the vintage only tends to be of vital importance when you're buying good-quality wines from areas such as Bordeaux and Burgundy.

MYTH 2: ALL WINES IMPROVE WITH AGE

Nonsense! The vast majority of wines—particularly whites—become increasingly dull and flaccid with age. Only very good-quality red wines, a few whites, and some Champagnes become softer and more attractive with age—and even that is very much a matter of personal taste. All other wines are made to be consumed in a year or two.

A love of rickety old wines—or "le vice anglais" as the French sometimes call it—is a peculiarly Anglo-Saxon obsession that has little to do with the pursuit of pleasure. Yes, some wonderfully mature wines do have a charm all of their own, but the vast majority are like anything else that has been lurking in a dark, dank cellar for a few years—pale and dusty.

If you like the flavor of old wines it isn't necessary to pay huge sums for them. Look out for the red Riojas that taste prematurely aged when they aren't more than four or five years old. There's more on Rioja in IDEA 24, *Spanish highs*.

Try another idea...

TASTE TEST

Old red Bordeaux is expensive, but for the purposes of this taste test you can keep costs down by choosing a wine that isn't from one of the star years. A trustworthy wine merchant will help. Try tasting:

- A cheap one- or two-year-old Cabernet-based red Bordeaux
- A ten- to fifteen-year-old Cabernet-based Bordeaux from a good vintage

"Appreciating old wine is like making love to a very old lady. It is possible. It can even be enjoyable. But it requires a bit of imagination."
ANDRE TCHELISTCHEFF

Defining idea...

How did it go?

Q I was amazed how well the red Bordeaux had aged. Do all wines from that region age in the same way?

A *Only the best-quality wines made in exceptional years. Ordinary red Bordeaux is like any other red wine: it will lose its character with age.*

Q Is it only wines from Bordeaux and Burgundy that age well?

A *No. There are plenty of wines from other areas, particularly Australia and California, that age well, too.*

Q You haven't made much mention of white wines. Is that because they don't really age?

A *Some people have a strange fascination with old white Burgundy, but almost all white wines are meant to be drunk when they're young. A notable exception is vintage Champagne, which ages beautifully.*

15

Words don't come easy

Though one can feel self-conscious when talking about wine, this is an essential part of deepening your understanding. Learn to do it with confidence—and without sounding like a wine bore.

Most of us find it difficult enough to describe a thought in our heads, let alone the contents of our glass.

Yet talking about wine and writing notes are stepping-stones on the path to becoming a free-thinking drinker. Sadly, the greatest obstacle that discourages the casual wine lover from talking meaningfully about wine is *fear*. Wine buffs have been so artfully parodied for so long that it is only natural to feel that any attempt to describe the flavor or aroma of a wine will make you sound like the most cringe-inducing caricature.

HAMMING IT UP

In recent years one major problem has been the producers of prime-time television programs who have sought to give wine appreciation widespread appeal by promoting experts whose crime is not just to ham up the subject by talking up the wines they taste—can a wine really smell of "freshly mown hay," "lychees," "summer

Here's an idea for you...

Wherever you go carry a notebook in which to write notes on the wine that you taste. You'll probably feel self-conscious about this at first, but friends and colleagues will soon get used to it.

hedgerows," and "barrels full of fruit?"—but also to make lesser mortals feel inhibited in their own attempts to talk about wine.

The first rule in talking and writing about wine is to try to avoid the sort of lengthy fanciful descriptions I've just alluded to. Although these might be useful to television presenters (they fill up more air time) and the authors of wine columns (they fill up more space), they do nothing but confuse the people who read them. Remember that wine appreciation is a wholly subjective field that is as open to interpretation as art or music. One wine lover's "gnat's pee" is another's "delightful hedgerow aromas." So it is essential to develop a personal vocabulary of your own rather than attempt to adopt someone else's.

Defining idea...

"When trying to talk about wine in depth, one rapidly comes up against the limitations of our means of expression . . . We need to be able to describe the indescribable. We tasters feel to some extent betrayed by language."
EMILE PEYNAUD

DEVELOPING YOUR OWN CODE

Because it isn't possible to be scientific about the way that a wine tastes or smells, I would always encourage you to develop your own opinions rather than simply take on the received views of others. If a wine book tells you that a certain type of wine tastes "nutty," there is a danger that nuttiness is what you'll think you've found, even if you haven't. So in your attempts to become more articulate about the contents of your wineglass it is a good idea to write notes using your *own* descriptions. What do the taste and smell of the wine remind you of? Compare the smell of a glass of Sauvignon Blanc, Pinot

Noir, or Chardonnay to some other familiar smell and its taste to a familiar flavor. Often the most meaningful descriptions aren't those that allude to some other flavor or aroma— sometimes they are as simple as "great length" or "tightly structured"—but, while I know what they mean, you may not, which is the reason it is essential to develop your own code.

Describing wines should become an intrinsic part of the taste tests you conduct. There's more on tasting in IDEA 5, *Put your palate through its paces.*

Try another idea...

WRITING NOTES

Focus on three key points: color, flavor, and aroma. Try to get into the habit of commenting on all three of these aspects of a wine—even if one or the other of them isn't especially noteworthy. When describing flavor, comparisons with fruits are popular, from the humble plum to the exotic lychee. But don't limit yourself to these. What about familiar flavors such as chocolate or licorice? Comparisons with flowers are useful when describing aromatic wines. But also think laterally. What about tobacco, wood smoke, or cedar? Note the intensity of the wine's color. Is it light, pallid, or opaque? It doesn't matter how fanciful your descriptions might seem; what's important is that they provide a useful shorthand to create a gastronomic word picture.

" 'When I use a word,' Humpty Dumpty said in rather a scornful tone, 'it means just what I choose it to mean— neither more nor less.' "
LEWIS CARROLL, *Alice in Wonderland*

Defining idea...

GO BOLDLY . . .

However inexperienced you are, you must have confidence in your opinions. Wine appreciation is an extremely subjective field, so your views are as valid as anyone else's.

How did it go?

Q Can the flavor and aroma of wine be compared to literally anything?

A   *As long as it means something to you. Try to limit yourself to a few well-chosen words rather than a whole string of them (known in the trade as "fruit salad tasting notes"). The aim is to create word pictures that trigger a memory. But there are times when just "good" or "bad" will suffice.*

Q If everyone develops their own personal wine-speak, doesn't talking about wine become rather pointless?

A   *Don't worry. All wine enthusiasts will eventually find some common ground.*

Q As a free-thinking drinker will I never be able to drink a wine without having an opinion about it?

A   *No. Can you imagine a football fanatic not having an opinion about a game of football?*

16

The heat is on

Temperature plays a key role in the way a wine expresses itself. Instead of adhering to prescriptive guidelines, throw away the rule book and discover what works best for you.

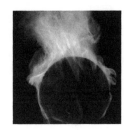

Wine buffs are very sensitive types. They're sensitive to smell and to taste, and they're particularly sensitive to temperature.

And often their approach to the temperature of wine is similar to a farmer's view of the weather—it's either too warm or too cold. This is a subject that can only really be explored with the help of some practical work, so before going any further I'm going to suggest a taste test.

TASTE TEST

- One glass of your favorite Champagne chilled until it is almost freezing + one glass of the same Champagne that is neither warm nor cold

COMPARE AND CONTRAST

The purpose of this test is to focus on the aroma and then the flavor of the wine in each of the glasses. Which has the greatest smell and which has the greatest flavor?

Here's an idea for you...

For a few days try to taste wines at different temperatures—not just in the formal environment of a taste test but also any time you happen to drink some wine. Keep the remnants of a bottle of red Bordeaux in the fridge and try it the next day. How does chilling affect Sauternes or Port? The more you experiment the more you'll be able to hone your judgment.

It's probably not often that you drink tepid Champagne—unless you're in the habit of cradling a glass of it in a sweaty palm—but to demonstrate the influence that temperature can have on a wine it is important to take two extremes.

Which of the two glasses had the most flavor? Which was the most refreshing? It's also worth trying the experiment with a variety of other wines, both red and white. You might find that the aroma and flavor of chilled red wines are similarly inert when compared with one another, but you might also find that there's something rather disgusting about wine that is the temperature of a warm bath.

The ability to judge the optimum temperature for a wine can be gained through a combination of common sense and experience in equal measure. For this reason there isn't much point in arming yourself with charts that dictate the ideal serving temperature of a wine. These will only tend to confuse you. For the free-thinking drinker, temperature is very much a question of personal taste.

TEMPERATURE TIPS FOR THE FREE-THINKING DRINKER

- The temperature of a bottle after it has been in the fridge for a few hours tends to be ideal.
- Putting a white wine in the freezer for a few minutes is a hopelessly inexact means of chilling it.

- If you want to chill a bottle of Champagne, do so in a bucket filled with ice and water rather than in the freezer. The latter will inevitably chill it until it is too cold, or worse still, waste the contents by freezing it.
- Similarly, the practice of placing a bottle of wine near a range cooker, stove, or radiator is a hopelessly imprecise way to get the wine to the correct temperature.
- The most ludicrous piece of advice on temperature is that some wines should be served at "room temperature." What sort of room? A centrally heated, hermetically sealed apartment? Or a chilly country house?

This might sound persnickety, but the temperature of the wine in your glass will depend on how you hold your glass and what sort of glass you're using. There's more on this subject in IDEA 6, *Scents and sensibilities*.

Try another idea...

COOL REDS

The idea that red wines should always be served a few degrees below tepid suggests that there are no red wines suitable for summer drinking. Nothing could be further from the truth. There are plenty of reds—such as Gamay and those from the Loire—that lend themselves to being served at the same temperature at which you would serve a dry white wine.

USING TEMPERATURE TO YOUR OWN ADVANTAGE

One of the most popular ruses employed by sneaky wine buffs to disguise substandard wine is to serve it in a carafe—so that it can "breathe" and its identity can't be identified—

"Drastic chilling subdues flavors—a useful ruse if you're serving basic wine, but a shame if the wine is very good."
OZ CLARKE

Defining idea...

at a temperature that is slightly warmer than it would normally be served. Even more cunning is to make sure that the wine—either red, white, or sparkling—is kept at such teeth chattering temperatures that it is almost impossible to detect its flavor—or lack of it. You'll be amazed at the beneficial effect it can have on all sorts of wines from the grimmest Muscadet to the most acidic Champagne.

How did it go?

Q   Why can chilling a red wine suppress its flavor?

A   *Partly because the temperature at which you serve a wine influences the way that the wine tastes and smells and also because the temperature changes your perception of it—cold can act like an anesthetic on the taste buds.*

Q   What makes a red wine suitable for chilling?

A   *If the wine has flavors that are pronounced enough to stand out despite a low temperature.*

Q   Are there any white wines that should be served slightly warmer than usual?

A   *Yes, but as a free-thinking drinker you should decide for yourself which ones.*

17

The reign of terroir

Is the idea of terroir nothing more than a figment of French winemakers' imaginations—a notion used as an excuse for badly made, earthy wines?

Or is it a valid concept that distinguishes great wines with a sense of place from those that are truly ordinary? You decide . . .

It might be easier to explain the term "terroir" if there were an English translation for it. It is a notion that encapsulates the French approach to wine, which they don't regard as simply an agricultural product but as a reflection of the climate, soil, topography, and geology of the area where the grapes were grown. The idea is tied up with the French belief that wine is primarily the gift of nature rather than of technology. As such, this notion is the polar opposite of the New World philosophy that wine is primarily the product of gleaming, temperature-controlled fermentation tanks.

To understand terroir it helps to look at it in the context of French gastronomy, the emphasis of which is on local ingredients. To the average French citizen, food is a reflection of the environment in which it was grown—and usually, thanks to a sense of regional pride, the meat, fruit, and vegetables produced locally are perceived as the best. The same goes for wine. Most French shoppers don't spend hours scratching their heads in a supermarket; they'll just buy whatever happens to be local. You also

Here's an
idea for
you...

If you need convincing about the influence that the weather and soil has on plant life, examine the difference in the flavors of the same variety of apples grown in different areas of the world.

rarely hear them talking about grape varieties. Wine is defined by where it comes from—Bordeaux, Loire, Rhône, Burgundy.

AN EXCUSE FOR POOR WINE?

To the detractors of traditional French winemaking, this attitude explains the poor quality of much of its output. French winemakers, they believe, simply plant the vines and let nature do the rest. The result is not just poor grapes but also limp, dirty-tasting wines. Although this might have been the approach of some winemakers in the dim past, it is certainly not true today. The truth is that it is quite possible to believe in both the concept of terroir and good winemaking.

The belief in terroir has spread beyond France. As winemaking in California, Australia, and South Africa becomes ever more sophisticated, winemakers are discovering that, far from being a far-fetched concept, terroir helps to explain the shades of difference between the wines made in different vineyards. So they are now identifying the areas that produce the best grapes—a practice that is having a huge impact on the quality of the wines. This is the reason that you'll now hear New World wine enthusiasts talking about "Barossa Shiraz," "Clare Valley Riesling," and "Carneros Pinot Noir" in much the same way that wine buffs of the old school talk about the pros and cons of specific areas such as Pauillac, Sancerre, and Condrieu.

Wines can be divided between those that express terroir and those that don't. In general, the more expensive the wine the more likely it is to offer sense of place. However, there are many exceptions to this rule: there are plenty of expensive wines that could be made anywhere in the world and plenty of cheap wines that eloquently express a sense of place.

TASTE TEST

- Good-quality Cabernet-based red Bordeaux + basic Chilean Cabernet

There's more discussion of the influence that the weather has on the character of wine in IDEA 13, _Come rain or shine._

Try another idea...

COMPARE AND CONTRAST

Which of these two wines do you feel owes most of its flavor to fruit? If one of the wines doesn't appear to have typically Cabernet-style characteristics, how would you describe its flavor and aroma?

Of course, the main reason that the wines taste different could be due to different winemaking techniques, but hopefully you will have seen the distinction between a wine that is essentially the product of the grape and one that has a sense of place.

FRUIT VERSUS TERROIR AND WINEMAKING TRADITION

"Man masters nature not by force but by understanding."
ROBERT BRIDGES

Defining idea...

All wines can roughly be split into the following four categories:

1. Those that express the flavor of the grapes they are made from
2. Those that express terroir
3. Those that express the winemaking tradition of the area where the wine was made
4. Those that express all of these

How did it go?

Q **Why is that you rarely find inexpensive wines that strongly suggest a sense of place?**

A *Largely because of the amount of intervention that takes place in the winery in order to compensate for the fact that the quality of the grapes isn't great.*

Q **I have noticed that some quite expensive wines don't really appear to have any regional characteristics. Why is this?**

A *Because they are a triumph of winemaking and blending over individuality. Often they are fashioned to compete in wine competitions rather than to appeal to consumers.*

Q **Are there any fresh, vibrant, fruity wines that also express terroir—or are the qualities mutually exclusive?**

A *You are more likely to find them in the southern hemisphere but the Loire Valley is a good hunting ground for them, too.*

18

In the mix

Making wines from just one type of grape might have made wine easier to understand, but many of the world's greatest wines are made from a blend of different grapes. It's time to decide whether you prefer your grapes straight or mixed.

New World winemakers might have created the current fashion for wines made from just one grape variety, but the habit isn't peculiar to them.

White Burgundy is made from Chardonnay, red Burgundy from Pinot Noir, and Loire whites from Sauvignon Blanc or Chenin Blanc. But a huge number of European wines—and an increasing number of New World wines—are made from blends. Most red Bordeaux is made from a blend, as are southern French reds and Champagne—not to mention a host of Spanish and Italian wines that are made from a number of different grapes.

Blending is about more than just mixing a lot of different wines together. It is a hugely complex art that involves using the different components to create just the right style. It's a skill not dissimilar to mixing paint colors to create precisely the right hue—and just as difficult.

Here's an idea for you... **To help you understand how different flavors combine together, focus on the taste of all the composite ingredients in a cocktail such as a Bloody Mary (tomato juice, vodka, Worcestershire sauce, lemon juice, pepper, salt, and celery salt) to see how different flavors react with one another.**

TASTE TEST: BLENDED REDS

Try the following lineup:
■ inexpensive Australian or Chilean Cabernet + New Zealand Pinot Noir + southern French blend + red Bordeaux blend

Before you reveal the identity of the wines see if you can tell which of them is made from just one grape and which are blended. Once you know what they are, compare the flavors and aromas of the blended and unblended wines.

TASTE TEST: BLENDED WHITES

White wines tend to be blended less frequently than reds, but there are an increasing number of delicious examples, including successful blends of Chardonnay and Sauvignon Blanc that combine the best of each grape's qualities. Perhaps the best-known example of a blended white is Champagne, which may include Chardonnay, Pinot Noir, and Pinot Meunier grapes.

Of almost any wine, non-vintage Champagne is the ultimate example of the blender's ability. It is perhaps because the climate of the Champagne region doesn't offer the ideal environment in which to grow grapes that producers have had to be extremely resourceful in making the best of what they have—a skill that is the key to blending. When blends are created in Champagne, wines from a variety of different vintages are painstakingly combined to make a wine that is not only attractive but also reflects the particular style of the Champagne house. When tasting a Champagne write a list of the grapes that have been used to create it and consider how they might have contributed to the flavor of the wine. In many cases, wines that might not have been very attractive on their own have combined to create a blend in which the sum is far, far greater than its parts.

THE CHANCE TO RIGHT WRONGS

But blending isn't just about creating good wines; it's also about avoiding making bad ones (a curious distinction, but you get the drift). Sometimes when winemakers blend wines they are compensating for the failings of one wine with the strengths of another. Another weapon in the blender's armory is blending not just wines made from different grapes but also wines from different regions and vintages to create a wine that is hopefully much better than the sum of its parts.

KEEP AN OPEN MIND

Though the modernists are naturally drawn to the simplicity of the idea of wines made from just one grape, even winemakers in the world's most progressive wine regions are discovering the joys of blending, particularly Bordeaux and Rhône style blends. The fact is that there isn't a right or a wrong approach. Some wines lend themselves to blending; others are better suited to a solo performance.

The reason that French winemakers are less focused on making wines from just one grape than are those in the southern hemisphere is partly because they believe that climate and soil are more important than the fruit on the vines. There's more on this in IDEA 17, *The reign of terroir*, and more on the importance of grapes in IDEA 10, *Grape expectations*.

Try another idea...

"Variety's the very spice of life, That gives all its flavor."
WILLIAM COWPER

Defining idea...

How did it go?

Q **If grapes are mixed, does their individual character become irrelevant?**

A   *To an extent—although in most cases there's one dominant grape.*

Q **Why is it that blended wines sometimes appear to have more layers of flavor and aroma than those made with just one grape variety?**

A   *Because combining the flavors of two or more grapes can create a wine with more character. That's the theory anyway. However, bear in mind that wines made from just one grape are sometimes lent other flavors—oak, for example—or they might gain more character with age. So in many cases the distinction between blended wines and those made from just one grape might not be obvious.*

Q **When matching food and wine, do blended wines and those made from one grape variety serve different purposes?**

A   *It can be a good idea to match wines with simple flavors to similarly simple foods (e.g., Muscadet and seafood) and those with complex flavors to complex foods (e.g., Rhône red with beef casserole).*

19

Cork talk

Once you know how, spotting corked wine is easy—but the fact is that you shouldn't have to.

Let's not go into how or why some wines are ruined by faulty corks. Let's just accept that it is a fate that, according to some statistics, affects one in every twelve bottles of wine that are sealed in this way.

The problem is not just this shocking statistic but the fact that most people so lack confidence in their opinions on wine that they are reluctant to complain about bottles that are afflicted with the fault. (Conversely, there are those who are so confident in their opinions that they dismiss almost everything they taste as being corked.)

Not being able to identify corkiness is not the huge misdemeanour that novice wine buffs fear. It takes time to learn to distinguish different characters in a wine—and corkiness is one of them. The mistake of confusing corkiness with oakiness, for example, isn't the heinous crime that it might seem. It isn't until you've tasted a half a dozen corked wines that their smell becomes so distinct.

Here's an idea for you... **Identifying the smell of wet cardboard will help you to sniff out corkiness. The best way to do this is to soak some cardboard in water overnight and put the pulp in a glass— breathe deeply and you will have a pretty good idea of what you are looking for.**

There are a variety of different euphemisms for corkiness. One of the most common is "musty," which isn't especially helpful because there are some wines—expensive red Rhônes, for example—that have that trait. A more useful comparison is wet cardboard.

Because corkiness is more evident in the aroma of a wine than in the flavor, most wine buffs simply need to sniff a wine to tell whether it is corked. It is for this reason that trying the wine is more than just a ritual (although one sometimes wonders why wine waiters don't test the wine themselves before serving it).

TASTE TEST

If you have an agreeable wine merchant or a friend who is knowledgeable about wine, ask them to save the next bottle of badly corked wine they come across so you can use it in the following test:

- corked white or red wine
- another bottle of the same wine in good condition

COMPARE AND CONTRAST

The glaring difference should imprint itself on your mind so indelibly that you couldn't fail to spot a corked wine in the future.

THE SIMPLE SOLUTION

What now makes the cork problem more galling is the fact that there's no longer any reason why white wines and everyday reds should ever be afflicted in this way. With the exception of high-quality reds intended for aging, which do benefit from their corks, all other wines should be fitted with metal screw caps that can simply be twisted off. Not only do such caps solve the problem of wines becoming corked, they also keep the wine fresher and more vibrant.

It is easy to confuse very oaky wine with corkiness. You'll find more on oakiness in IDEA 12, *Waiter, there's some oak in my glass.*

Try another idea...

THE PROBLEM OF PERCEPTIONS

The only reason that screw caps haven't caught on more rapidly is prejudice. The fact that they are still associated with cheap wines means that many people would prefer to run the risk of drinking faulty wine. Moreover, many drinkers prefer the ritual of pulling a cork rather than the less romantic business of twisting a metal cap.

THE TORTUOUS CORK DEBATE

If only the argument over corks was as simple as presented here. In fact, there are a variety of twists and turns in the debate. One of the key issues is the impact the demise of cork is having on rural areas of Portugal, which is traditionally the biggest source of the wood. The effect is more than just economic; environmentalists also point out that the rise of

"The difference in a trial of wine by the consumer and the expert is that the former seeks for something agreeable, something to praise; whilst the latter seeks for a fault, a blemish, or something to condemn."
ARPAD HARASZTHY

Defining idea...

81

the screw cap will spell the end of the rare Iberian lynx that live in cork forests. Then there is the issue of plastic corks that have also been touted as being a good solution to the problem. As with all issues relating to wine the sensible answer is to be guided by your taste buds and your olfactory system—but who knows? Perhaps your ecological concerns might also get the better of you.

DON'T BECOME A CORK BORE

It is not uncommon for hardened wine buffs to send back two or three bottles of wine that they believe to be corked or faulty. Not every wine is perfect. If corkiness smacks you in the face then do send it back, but don't try to act smart by finding fault in everything.

How did it go?

Q   Will wine shops exchange corky wine?

A   *Yes, most wine shops are happy to exchange corked wines, particularly if it means keeping a valued customer.*

Q   Are screw caps becoming more common?

A   *Yes, particularly on wines from New Zealand, where freshness is key. There are some wineries that now only produce wines sealed in this way, so if you want to drink their wines you'll have to overcome any prejudices you might have.*

20

Counting on Cabernet

Cabernet Sauvignon has been used to make some of the world's most expensive, long-lived wines—and also some of the most disappointing. Find the best examples and you could be in for a lifelong love affair.

Cabernet Sauvignon, like Chardonnay, is a wine about which it is virtually impossible to make any sweeping generalizations.

There are few similarities, for example, between a simple, fruity Chilean Cabernet made last year and a ten-year-old Cabernet-based red Bordeaux that has lain evolving in its bottle in some deep, dark cellar. What many Cabernets tend to do, however, is make wines with an attractive three-dimensional quality that are approachable when young—and, in some cases, sufficiently robust to age beautifully. For these reasons Cabernet is often used in blended wines, either with Merlot or to give body to wines such as Chianti.

A SHORT HISTORY OF CABERNET

Our ancestors drank copious amounts of Cabernet without knowing it. The grape is the mainstay of many red Bordeaux, particularly those from areas such as the hallowed Medoc (although the name of the grape would never have appeared on

Here's an idea for you... **You might like to try comparing some examples of Cabernet with a Merlot, Shiraz, Pinot Noir, or red Rioja. The more you try the better, because doing so will highlight not just the differences but also the similarities. Each new comparison will help you to build up a crystal-clear profile in your mind of Cabernet's place in the vinous world.**

the label). From the sixteenth century, Cabernet was a drink for which the British had an almost unquenchable thirst, and it was exported all over the Empire. The grape's recent history pretty much mirrors that of Chardonnay. With the rise of New World winemakers, Cabernet was planted the length and breadth of the southern hemisphere and used to produce wines that were rather different in style, largely because of the combination of new winemaking techniques and a warmer climate. Now the grape is as ubiquitous as Chardonnay, making fabulous long-lived wines everywhere from Bordeaux to the Barossa.

THE FLAVOR OF CABERNET

One of the reasons for the success of Australian and Chilean wines, particularly Cabernet, is that winemakers in these countries succeeded in giving them a dose of sometimes imperceptible sweetness that made them more approachable than those from Cabernet's spiritual home in Bordeaux. Like oakiness, sweetness is one of those qualities that is perfectly palatable in a wine when it is balanced with some other pronounced flavor, such as acidity. Ask any chef and they will tell you that similar balancing acts are essential to the success of all sorts of dishes. Imagine a hot spicy curry without chutney, or a Chinese main course that is sweet but not sour.

CABERNET AND FOOD

One of the reasons for the success of Cabernet, besides its approachable flavors, is its affinity with a wide variety of different foods. From a classic combination such as mature Cabernet-based red Bordeaux with roast lamb to juicy New World Cabernet with grilled meats, it is a gregarious mixer. Because, like Chardonnay, Cabernet has a variety of different incarnations, you simply have to match its various styles with the right foods. Dishes with subtle flavors call for a similarly subtle accompaniment, whereas those with a bolder character can stand up to something a little more assertive. Remember that fruity flavors in a wine are an ideal match for dishes, such as turkey, that are traditionally served with fruity sauces.

TASTE TEST

- Expensive Cabernet-based Bordeaux that is no less than five years old
- Inexpensive Chilean Cabernet
- Bulgarian Cabernet
- Californian Cabernet
- Inexpensive Cabernet-based South African blend

If you want to learn how Cabernet ages, turn to IDEA 14, *Growing old gracefully*, which includes a taste test that compares a young Cabernet-based red Bordeaux with a ten-year-old example.

Try another idea...

"Burgundies, on the whole, do not keep as long as clarets; they have more to give, more bouquet and greater vinosity, at first, but they exhaust themselves and fade away sooner than the less aromatic, more reserved clarets. It is somewhat like some of the carnations, which possess a far more pungent and assertive perfume, when first picked, than any rose; yet the more discreet, the gentler and sweeter perfume of the rose will abide with the bloom as long as the bloom will last."
ANDRE L. SIMON

Defining idea...

COMPARE AND CONTRAST

Consider the color, aroma, flavor, whether some of the wines were sweeter than others, and how the wines that include only Cabernet compare with those in which Cabernet has been blended with another grape variety. Think about how each wine would go with food. Would you prefer to drink them on their own? If you choose to drink them with food, what kind of food do you think they would go well with?

How did it go?

Q   The wine that really stood out was the red Bordeaux. Why is this?

A   *There are a number of reasons for this:*
  ■ *The climate in Bordeaux rarely allows grapes to ripen as much they might in areas such as Chile or Australia, so the red wines of Bordeaux tend to be more restrained in style.*
  ■ *A few years in the bottle may have softened the rather hard, robust character of the wine when it was first made.*
  ■ *In Bordeaux, Cabernet is often blended with another grape—frequently Merlot—that would have softened its character.*

Q   A couple of the wines seem really quite tough and chewy compared with others that had an easier, fruitier character. How do you account for that?

A   *It's probably because they are younger. Also, there are some parts of the world—Eastern Europe and South Africa, for example—where robust styles of wine are popular. If these wines seem very assertive try to imagine drinking them with a hearty goulash or some South African barbecued beef. Better still, don't just imagine it—try it!*

21

Bordeaux, Burgundy, and Champagne

How to enjoy classic French wines—and avoid those that are a triumph of flash over flavor.

Imagine. You're standing in a wine shop with a credit card in your hand, prepared to pay handsomely for a wine that will impress a host who doesn't know much about wine but is extremely label conscious.

Before you on the shelves are ranks of expensive bottles not just from France but also from Australia, New Zealand, California, and Chile. But the likelihood is that it is not the latter you are drawn to but the premier crus and grand crus classes in swirly script. However superior the contents of the bottles from the southern hemisphere, the names "Chablis," "Medoc," or "Champagne" on a bottle have a far higher perceived value than "Barossa," "Napa," or "Maipo." Sad but true. If you want to achieve the status of free-thinking drinker this is a situation that requires work.

Here's an idea for you...

Sadly, there aren't many opportunities to taste top-notch Bordeaux, Burgundy, and Champagne without investing in whole bottles. However, many specialist wine merchants hold wine dinners that, although quite expensive, do allow you to taste a variety of well-chosen, good-quality wines at one sitting. Why not give one a whirl?

THE HARD FACTS

Whatever the skills of winemakers in the southern hemisphere, they have so far failed to cloak their wines in the mystique for which most of us seem so happy to pay. Regardless of their quality, many wines from Bordeaux, Burgundy, and Champagne sell for two or three times more than wines from elsewhere that are arguably much better. What complicates this situation further is that as well as creating some terrible, pleasure-free wines, these three areas also happen to be sources of some of the most magnificent wines known to humankind. In order to defend yourself against exploitation you need to know a few facts:

1. Inexpensive Bordeaux, Burgundy, or Champagne is almost certain to be pretty grim (unless it's stolen). Your money would almost certainly be much better spent in southern France, Germany, Italy, or the New World.
2. It is possible to find delicious, affordable wines from Bordeaux, Burgundy, and Champagne, but it requires a great deal of work—which will be more than repaid with wonderful, subtle flavors that are hard to find elsewhere.
3. It isn't all bad news. High-quality Champagne is one of the world's best-value wines—even when it costs as much as a decent pair of shoes.

GETTING TO KNOW THE WINES

For most people the cost of a tasting that would help you explore the subtleties of the finest Bordeaux, Burgundy, and Champagne is prohibitive. Instead, you should treat the matter as a lifetime's journey. Bordeaux alone has almost a quarter of a million acres of vineyard and almost 13,000 producers—so it could take you a lifetime just to come to grips with the wines of this region, let alone those from Burgundy and Champagne.

Are you getting a taste for the subtleties of Bordeaux, Burgundy, and Champagne? There's more on each in IDEA 23, *Lovely bubbly?*, IDEA 44, *The great Burgundy test*, and IDEA 46, *Break for the Bordeaux*.

Try another idea...

The more you taste wines from all over the world, the greater your opportunities to put those from Bordeaux, Burgundy, and Champagne into context. At their very best, they have a restraint, subtlety, and complexity that you will soon discover is a rare quality outside of Europe (at their worst, you will wonder how they ever found their way into a bottle). They also have a capacity to age gracefully.

However, unlike wine from most other regions, you really have to be prepared to dig deep in your pockets for the best examples. The good news is that Bordeaux, Burgundy, and Champagne by no means have a monopoly on the qualities with which they are traditionally associated. The wonderfully fragile, raspberry-ish character of fine Burgundy and the cedary aromas of red Bordeaux can now also be found in wines from elsewhere, notably Spain, California, and New Zealand. The one exception is Champagne. Though sparkling wines from areas such as the Loire, northern Italy, and Australia tend to be infinitely better quality than cheap Champagne, it is rare to taste examples that come close to the complexity and wonderful bready aromas of top-notch Champagne.

"Failure is not the only punishment for laziness; There is also the success of others."
JULES RENARD, French writer

Defining idea...

THE QUESTION OF COST

Although it might appear that producers in Bordeaux, Burgundy, and Champagne are guilty of charging extortionate prices compared with their counterparts in the southern hemisphere, in many cases they have little choice: The inflated price of land in prestigious areas coupled with the relatively high cost of labor and intensive winemaking techniques means that it is expensive to make wines such as these. As a free-thinking drinker, you will have to decide whether it is a price worth paying.

How did it go?

Q **Why is it that even quite expensive white Burgundy has a thin, mean character that leaves me cold?**

A *Probably because you are used to the slightly sweeter, sunnier characters of white wines from the southern hemisphere.*

Q **Are cheap wines from Bordeaux, Burgundy, and Champagne to be avoided at all costs?**

A *Extensive tasting will allow you to answer this question. The key is never to favor a bottle of wine from any of these three areas just because of their prestige.*

Q **Why is it so difficult to find top-notch sparkling wine outside Champagne?**

A *So far there have been few attempts to challenge Champagne's supremacy. The best attempt is one made in a part of Britain that has soil and climate very similar to those in Champagne.*

22

The beautiful south

A hitchhiker's guide to the deep, inky reds and three-dimensional whites of southern France.

This huge slice of France stretches all the way from the Pyrenees to the Alps and encompasses a vast variety of areas including Corbieres, Fitou, Limoux, Minervois, Luberon, and St. Chinian (as well as the unfortunately named La Clape and Coteaux de Pierrevert).

These areas are home to thousands of producers making a multitude of different styles of wine. Unlike other sizeable regions such as Australia and Chile, you won't have the comfort of exploring it from the perspective of a handful of well-known varieties such as Chardonnay, Sauvignon, Cabernet, and Merlot. Of course, these grapes do grow in the South of France but what makes the region's wines so compelling is a host of other grapes such as Carignan, Cinsaut, Mourverde, Grenache, Rolle, Roussanne, and Marsanne. These rarely make solo appearances in wine. Instead, they are used in diverse combinations to make blends. Though this fact might make the area seem daunting to wine lovers weaned on single-variety

Here's an idea for you...

Find a map that covers the South of France in detail. Whenever you taste a wine from the region try to find the place where it was made. Soon you'll have a clear picture of the complex geography of the region.

wines (from winemaking regions whose names we know how to pronounce), it also helps to make the region's wines so beguiling.

Another attraction of the South of France is that it is almost the antithesis of the corporate, marketing-obsessed wine industries to be found in California, Australia, and Chile. Although multinational companies have been attracted to the region in recent years, many of its best winemakers are small producers ekeing out a living by making handmade wines with love and care. If you are looking for romance in wine, then you will find it here.

GETTING TO KNOW THE WINES

How does one begin to tackle an area as vast as the South of France? The answer is with an open mind. Leave all your preconceptions at the door and search the region's highways and byways for new flavors and aromas. Yes, you might often be disappointed, but for every dull wine you taste you'll find half a dozen winners.

So vast is the number of different wines—and the variety of styles—that even a blind tasting of a hundred wines would hardly scratch the surface. What is essential is to try to put the wines in context. How does one of the wonderful reds from an area such as Costieres de Nimes, made from a hodgepodge of grapes such as Grenache Noir, Syrah, Carignan, Mourverde, and Cinsaut, compare with a Chilean or South African equivalent made from just one—say, Cabernet, Merlot, or Shiraz? Is it better or worse? Which would you rather drink with food?

Also, don't overlook the whites. The South of France might be better known for its reds and rosés, but there are also plenty of whites that will revive anyone with a palate that's been worn out by oaky Chardonnays and assertive Sauvignons—vibrant, tangy whites such as Picpoul de Pinet.

The South of France is the region that offers the most convincing evidence of why blending can create fabulous wines. You'll find more on this subject in IDEA 18, *In the mix.*

Try another idea...

A SHORT HISTORY OF SOUTHERN FRENCH WINES

Wine has been made in southern France since before the Roman invasion of Gaul. In the middle ages winemaking thrived under the influence of the monastic system. In the nineteenth century the region's fortunes rose with the advent of railways that connected it to lucrative markets in the north—and fell with the arrival of phylloxera, a disease that ravages vines. In the twentieth century the dominance of the cooperative system encouraged apathy and the region became associated with indifferent vin du pays. Lately, however, the area has seen a renaissance with the arrival of winemakers who are passionate about their craft and attracted to inexpensive land and a temperate climate.

"Oh for a beaker of the warm South
Full of the true, the blushful Hippocrene,
With beaded bubbles winking at the brim,
And purple-stained mouth;
That I might drink, and leave the world unseen,
And with thee fade away into the forest dim."
JOHN KEATS

Defining idea...

93

How did it go?

Q As you suggested, I have taken a random approach to tasting southern French reds but, having become used to the flavors and aromas of familiar names such as Cabernet and Merlot, I have to admit that I was flummoxed by the unusual wines that I tried. Why is this?

A *Your confusion is completely understandable. In order for you to learn about—and to appreciate—the wines of the South of France you need to cut loose from your reliance on the grapes to understand that wines are more than just alcoholic fruit juice. The more you taste, the more you'll realize that they are also expressions of the winemaker's art and the areas where they are made.*

Q Would it help my understanding if I tried to find single-variety examples of wines made from Grenache, Mourvedre, and Syrah?

A *There would be very little mileage in doing so. Southern French wines are infinitely greater than the sum of their parts.*

Q Why did some of the reds seem a little coarse compared with the softer reds that I am used to?

A *Possibly because you weren't drinking them with food.*

23

Lovely bubbly?

Although many people regard fizzy wine as a treat, there's no doubt that bubbles can mask some pretty tawdry, hangover-inducing wines.

If there is a gene that determines self-belief there must be a great deal of it swilling around in the gene pool of the Champenois.

But these masters of the art of blowing one's own trumpet are curiously quiet when it comes to the question of why their ancestors were so keen to fill their wines with bubbles. Though it might be a very impressive feat of oenological skill, there isn't an obvious reason to do it. Or is there? Maybe all those bubbles served as a good distraction from the sharp, unripe character of the wines produced in the chilly climes of northern France. The problem is that many people forget that sparkling wine—and Champagne, in particular—for all the fancy foil and livery is nothing more than a wine and its success or failure depends not on the bubbles but on the wine used to make it.

For proof you simply need to keep a glass of leftover sparkling wine or Champagne in a fridge until it is flat. Stripped of its bubbles what does it taste like when compared with your favorite white? The answer to this question will not only provide an insight into the quality of the wine but also help to deepen your understanding of sparkling wines.

Here's an idea for you... **Drinking a bad Champagne is as instructive as drinking a delicious example. When you taste a bad Champagne don't dismiss it immediately; struggle on to the end of the glass so that you can identify that it really is bad. The next good glass will taste all the more delicious.**

However tempting it might be to denigrate sparkling wines from Champagne, in my own experience the sparkling wines that taste best when flat have all been from its hallowed soil. That said, the region is also the birthplace of an equal number of unutterably disgusting wines.

WHAT'S IN A NAME?

So successfully have the Champenois marketed their wares—and guarded their name—that many people regard Champagne and sparkling wine as two completely different drinks. In fact, Champagne is simply a sparkling wine—albeit a rather fancy one.

TASTE TEST 1

- Expensive vintage Champagne
- Grand Marque Champagne
- Cheap Champagne (the cheapest you can find)
- Mid-price Australian sparkling wine
- Proscecco

COMPARE AND CONTRAST

This should prove to be a fascinating tasting. First, serve all the wines together and record your observations, especially on the differences between the various wines. You could also give marks out of ten for flavor and aroma. Take your time with this and remember that what you are tasting is a wine. Don't be distracted by either the bubbles or your preconceptions. Next, reveal the wines' identities and prices and compare them with your marks. It would also be a very useful exercise to put all the wines in the fridge for a couple of days and try them again when they are flat.

The subject of whether French wines such as Champagne are a triumph of flash over flavor is explored further in IDEA 21, Bordeaux, Burgundy, and Champagne.

Try another idea...

THE ORIGINS OF CHAMPAGNE

Because the Champagne region is so cold, fermentation of wine often stopped in the winter and didn't restart again until the spring, causing wines to become highly carbonated. The market for Champagne was kick-started in the eighteenth century when stronger bottles and reinforced corks allowed the fizziness to be marketed as a virtue rather than a vice.

STYLE GUIDE

"Come quickly, I'm tasting stars."
DOM PERIGNON, on discovering Champagne

Defining idea...

- *Non-vintage.* Most of the Champagne we drink is non-vintage that is made from a blend of wines from two or more years. The fact that it is blended allows the wine to have a consistent style.
- *Vintage.* A Champagne made from wines from just one very good year. Vintage status is no guarantee of quality, since what constitutes a "good year" is debatable.
- *Blanc de blanc.* Champagne made from Chardonnay.
- *Blanc de noirs.* Champagne made from Pinot Noir and/or Pinot Meunier.
- *Rosé.* Pink Champagne made from black grapes, or ordinary Champagne colored with red wine.

TASTE TEST 2

This one is quite simple. Buy an example of each Champagne listed above and compare them blind.

How did it go?

Q **I was fascinated that—with a few exceptions—there appeared to be little correlation between the cost of the bottles and their contents. Am I missing something?**

A   *No, you're not. Perhaps more than any other wine, sparkling wine is sold on perception rather than quality.*

Q **Why does Champagne tend to be so expensive?**

A   *Everything in Champagne is expensive, from the land to the expertise. Add to that the huge marketing and advertising costs plus the fact that sitting on all those vintage wines until they are released will burn a sizeable hole in your balance sheet. However, in some cases, it is a price worth paying.*

Q **I noticed that Prosecco is considerably more palatable than many of the inexpensive Champagnes and sparkling wines I've tasted. Is there any particular reason for this?**

A   *The main reason is that most Proseccos have a subtle, fruity sweetness that takes the edge off the acidity and makes this wine much more approachable than Champagne. Prosecco also has the attraction of being a fraction of the price.*

24

Spanish highs

Don't ignore Spanish wines just because their labels seem more confusing than those from the New World. Spain produces some of the world's most seductive wines, and they cost a fraction of the price of comparable wines from more fashionable regions.

Spain offers a rich seam for wine lovers on the hunt for character and value for money.

The country's wines—which range from delicious, mature-tasting red Riojas to heady, awe-inspiring Fino sherries—are almost the antithesis of the easy, fruit-driven offerings from Australia, Chile, and South Africa. The result is that—like wines from unfashionable European wine regions such as southern France, Italy, and Germany—they require a different approach than to the wines from the southern hemisphere. Nevertheless, the rewards are great for those prepared to forget about consistency, clear labeling, and familiar grapes—and to set off to explore the highs and lows that Spain has to offer.

In the late 1970s, Spanish wine—particularly Rioja—came within a hair's breadth of being fashionable. Stratospheric red Bordeaux prices were France's loss and Spain's gain. But just as Spanish wines were beginning to enjoy their newfound respectability, so, too, were Australian wines that were more approachable and offered better value. Whatever the claims that renewed energy and investment

Here's an
idea for
you... **Spain's wine regions are as
complex as those in the South
of France. As you try the wines,
plot their position on a map of
Spain. This discipline helps
focus the mind and you'll
discover all sorts of places that
you never knew existed.**

would enable Spain's winemakers to compete,
Spanish wines still present something of a
minefield to the casual buyer. As you may have
realized by now, a casual buyer's minefield is
the free-thinking drinker's gold mine.

ORIENTATION TOUR—REDS

Because Spanish wines are so varied in style,
starting your tour with a scattershot approach will help you find the styles you like.
Over a period of a few weeks taste as many reds as you can from the two areas best
known for their red wines: Rioja and Ribera del Duero. Having identified your
favorites from each area, taste them again alongside other reds that you know well. A
possible lineup could include: Ribera del Duero × 2, Rioja × 2, Chilean Cabernet
Sauvignon, a southern French red, Rhône red, and a good mature red Bordeaux.

COMPARE AND CONTRAST

The joy of this taste test is that you will be comparing some wines that couldn't be
more different—not just because they are made from different grapes but also
because of the climate and landscape where they were produced. Nevertheless, the
chances are that alongside the differences you'll also find some surprising similarities.

ORIENTATION TOUR—WHITES

Take a similar approach with the whites. Again, start with Rioja. Try a handful of
whites before moving on to Galicia, the region in the windswept northwestern
extremity of Spain, where you should try any Albarinos you can lay your hands on.

Finally, select your two favorite wines from each area. For your taste test you might then compare: white Rioja × 2, Albarino × 2, New Zealand Sauvignon, good oaky Australian Chardonnay, Muscadet, and Verdicchio.

The wine that is conspicuous by its absence from this section is Sherry—one of the greatest of all Spanish wines. You'll find out about Sherry in IDEA 30, Sherry baby.

Try another idea...

COMPARE AND CONTRAST

As in France, the focus of the winemaker is on style rather than grapes—of which there are almost 600 different varieties in Spain. From a weeding out perspective the only grapes you need to concern yourself with are Tempranillo, used to make red wines in Ribera del Duero, and Garnacha—the grape that the French call "Grenache Noir." The two white grapes to focus on initially are Albarino and Viura, the grape in white Rioja.

TYPICAL VERSUS MODERN

When selecting wines from European regions such as Spain you're faced with a choice between those that are "typical"—i.e., they adhere to a style that is true to the region where they are made—and those that are "modern," which seek to mimic the styles of wine from the southern hemisphere. There is nothing intrinsically wrong with the latter, but in the interest of deepening your knowledge of Spanish wines it makes sense to avoid them.

"There is something about the unexpected that moves us. As if the whole of existence is paid for in some way, except for that one moment, which is free."
ROSE TREMAIN, British writer

Defining idea...

101

Q   Why is it that some of the Riojas tasted quite mature despite the fact they were from recent vintages?

A   *This is probably thanks to the Tempranillo grape. The quality you've noticed is one that helps explain Rioja's success as an alternative to red Bordeaux in the '70s.*

Q   I wasn't impressed with the Albarino. It lacked the fruitiness that I like in white wine. Is this my fault or the wine's?

A   *Albarino is an acquired taste. Think of it as Spain's answer to Muscadet. Like Muscadet, it is delicious with fish and seafood.*

Q   Why is it that many of the Riojas were either too thin or too heavy?

A   *Either through bad winemaking or because that is the way the winemakers like them. When you find a Rioja that you like, stick with it. The only problem you will then face is that the styles can vary enormously from year to year.*

25

A user's guide to sommeliers

So you find the people who serve wine in restaurants patronizing and unnecessary? You clearly haven't read the operating manual . . .

A few years ago there was an urban myth concerning sommeliers. Like all urban myths, it was unlikely that it was true—but like all urban myths it served to highlight a deep-seated collective neurosis.

The story concerned a man who took a date to a fancy French restaurant in an attempt to impress her. Once the waiter had taken their food order the male diner asked him to suggest a wine. "Would you like the sommelier?" asked the waiter. "Yes, please," said the diner with enthusiasm. "I've heard that's delicious!"

The point of this tale is that if you can make a fool of yourself even *before* you've been ministered to by the sommelier, what hope would you have when he's arrived? To be fair to sommeliers, the caricature is based on a breed that is now largely extinct—big, surly men with curious little silver cups known as tastevins hanging around their necks.

Here's an idea for you... **The next time you are faced with a sommelier, try to give them as wide an opening as possible. There are few things that a sommelier loves more than to think laterally and offer creative suggestions that might broaden your horizons. Try not to specify the wine that you want, or else at least pitch your request in the form of "red Bordeaux or something similar in style."**

These days, they tend to be young wine enthusiasts brimming with knowledge that they are eager to share with customers.

Whatever your level of knowledge, the advantage of using a sommelier is that they know the wines on their lists like the backs of their hands—from background information about the winery to the intimate details of the vintages. Better still, their art is to suggest which wines will go best with your choice of food. The best sommeliers are those who are able to educate their customers, not by firing reams of information at them but by broadening their vinous horizons with suggestions of wines that they might not otherwise have been brave enough to try. In a few cases, sommeliers have gone on to become wine superstars such as Gerard Basset of the British Hotel du Vin chain and Kevin Zraly of Windows on the World restaurant, which, until September 11, 2001, sat atop one of the towers of the World Trade Center. Both were as much a part of the unique selling point of their respective establishments as the chefs.

SOME TIPS ON SOMMELIERS

Don't be afraid of sommeliers. Most are passionate about their subject and eager to share their knowledge. If you are at a restaurant primarily to enjoy the food rather than to do business, their advice is likely to enhance your enjoyment.

One of the dangers of following the advice of a sommelier is that they may be eager to push wines with a high profit margin. Although you might not wish to appear mean by asking the price, tread with care and if you feel uncertain, take a surreptitious look at the list before ordering.

The purpose of a good sommelier is to enhance your enjoyment of the food by suggesting a wine that will go well with it. There's more on matching food and wine in IDEA 33, *The secret of a happy marriage.*

Try another idea...

If the sommelier suggests a wine that you know you don't like, don't be afraid to ask for other suggestions.

If you discover a sommelier you like and trust, try to make that restaurant a regular haunt. The more a sommelier understands your likes and dislikes, the more fruitful the relationship will be.

WINE LISTS

If you find the idea of a sommelier too intimidating your other resource should be the restaurant's wine list. These should do more than simply offer the name and price of a bottle of wine—the best can be extremely informative, with background information on wines and their vintages. The test of a really excellent list is that it should include enough information to offer a lone diner an evening of entertainment.

"The wise man is not the man who gives the right answers: he is the one who asks the right questions."
CLAUDE LEVI STRAUSS

Defining idea...

THE PRICE CONSPIRACY THEORY

Those who are suspicious of restaurateurs and their practices claim that the reason wine lists include so many offbeat wines is not because a sommelier wants to offer variety but because it makes it easier to charge for them. The idea is that we are less likely to mind paying a 400 percent markup on a little-known wine than on one that is available at a wine merchant.

How did it go?

Q **My biggest fear when dealing with a sommelier is that I will end up ordering something beyond my budget. How do I avoid this?**

A *One solution is to give a hint by pointing out a wine of the sort of price you want to pay and say, "I was thinking of having this wine but do you have any suggestions of comparable wines?" The sommelier would have to be pretty unscrupulous to suggest something much more expensive.*

Q **Do all restaurants have sommeliers?**

A *No. Most high quality restaurants do. Sometimes you will just have a knowledgeable waiter. And in others there are only waiters who know nothing at all about wine.*

Q **What is the best plan if the waiter appears to know nothing about wine?**

A *Either go for a wine that you know well or, if the wine list has plenty of explanatory notes, follow those.*

26

The wizards of Aus

Do Australian winemakers make wines that are fresh, vibrant, and fruity or dull, boring, and a triumph of marketing? It's time to make up your mind in the great Australian wine debate.

Let's start with the heart of the debate, which can be summarized as follows.

THE CASE FOR AUSTRALIA

- Big, consistent, fruit-driven wines.
- Labels that are easy to understand.

AND THE CASE AGAINST

- Australia produces dull, predictable, fruit-driven wines.
- The wines are overpriced in comparison with other countries in the southern hemisphere, where costs are cheaper, and also with most European wine regions.

For the free-thinking drinker, the answer should be to keep an open mind and remember that the most convincing orators in a debate such as this are the wines themselves. Wine buffs are prone to making sweeping generalizations about wine,

Here's an idea for you...

You'll gain a better insight into Australian wine if you have a good understanding of the country's food. Find a book on Australian cooking that will give you a good idea of the typically pronounced flavors created with gutsy ingredients such as garlic, apricots, oranges, capers, and figs.

but inevitably their arguments are riddled with exceptions—particularly in relation to Australia. Yes, it's easy to become bored by the rather homogeneous style of some Australian wines (as it is by some of the thin, mean wines produced in France, Spain, and Italy), but there will also be times when that type of wine is precisely what you want. There is also a sense in which Australian winemakers are victims of their own success; the country's wines have become popular so rapidly that many people treat them with the same suspicious approach they took to Japanese cars in the 1970s.

But there is also no doubt that the pioneering spirit of Australian winemakers has made them masters of innovation who have recently achieved great things with obscure, offbeat grape varieties such Verdelho and Gewürztraminer that have been unloved and overlooked by others. Indirectly, they have also improved the general standard of European wines.

A SHORT HISTORY OF AUSTRALIAN WINE

Palatable wine has been made in Australia since the early nineteenth century, but Australian wine as we know it has its roots in the '50s. Although many Australians at that time had a taste for sweet, heavily fortified wine (and beer), the emergence over the next two decades of good-quality dry styles of table wine slowly transformed tastes. In addition, the arrival of classic European grape varieties created wines with international appeal. The rest, as they say, is history.

TASTE TEST

This test assumes that you are by now pretty familiar with everyday Australian Chardonnays and Cabernets. It makes sense to explore the best quality examples you can afford as well as those that Australia has almost made its own, such as Semillon and Shiraz.

THE REDS

These are wines that you probably already know but for the purpose of this idea it makes sense to taste them alongside certain European wines. Try good-quality Coonawarra Cabernet, Barossa Shiraz, red Bordeaux, and Rhône red. The following combinations will be particularly instructive:

- Good-quality Coonawarra Cabernet + good-quality red Bordeaux
- Good-quality Barossa Shiraz + good-quality Rhône red

THE WHITES

Try the following combinations:
- Hunter Valley Chardonnay + good white Burgundy
- Clare Valley Riesling + German Riesling
- Good-quality Semillon + Semillon-based white Bordeaux
- Western Australian Sauvignon + Loire Sauvignon

One of the reasons that some people are critical of Australian wines is that they feel that these wines don't sufficiently express the soil and climate of where they were produced. There's more on this topic in IDEA 17, *The reign of terroir*.

Try another idea...

"In a climate so favorable, the cultivation of vines may doubtless be carried to a degree of perfection."
CAPTAIN ARTHUR PHILLIP, commander of the fleet that carried the first British settlers to Sydney in 1788

Defining idea...

109

You will have noticed the taste test includes wines that come from specific areas such as the Hunter Valley, the Barossa, Coonawarra, and Western Australia. As the Australian wine industry has grown ever more sophisticated, winemakers are learning more about which grapes respond best to which areas.

The result is that there is a new emphasis on regionality that mirrors the French obsession with terroir. The more you explore Australian wines, the more you'll discover these regional differences. The more you learn, the more you'll realize that anyone who makes generalizations about Australian wines is sure to be an imposter.

Q **I found the style of some of the Australian wines quite overpowering. Is this a common trait of Australian wines?**

How did it go?

A *Yes, Australian wines tend to be pretty supercharged compared with European wines made with the same grape varieties. This is partly to do with climate and partly to do with winemaking—and it's the way that Australians like them. Remember that big blockbuster wines such as Barossa Shiraz are intended to be drunk with hearty fare.*

Q **So is it essential to drink these wines with food?**

A *Very robust reds are best with food, but very aromatic whites such as Riesling, Sauvignon, and Semillon also make excellent, palate-reviving aperitifs.*

Q **I was under the impression that Australian wines are all about expressing grape varieties and European ones are all about expressing terroir. Can Australian wines really do both?**

A *Yes, there is a sense in which Australian wines can offer you the best of both worlds. But in Europe wines that express terroir tend to have more restrained, earthy qualities than the wine from down under.*

111

27

Fantasy island

Thirty years ago the idea that New Zealand would one day become a source of some of the world's best-quality white wines would have been treated with a loud guffaw among wine buffs. Lamb, yes, but world-class Sauvignon Blanc, Pinot Noir, Riesling, and Pinot Gris? Give us a break!

What has been extraordinary about New Zealand's story is not just the speed with which its wines have emerged on the world stage but also the way that it has succeeded more than any other New World region in beating the French at their own game.

While Loire producers complacently churned out Sauvignon Blancs that relied more on their name than their flavor, the New Zealanders set about making their own Sauvignons that delivered punchy, vibrant freshness almost eye-watering in its intensity.

Here's an idea for you... **Try tasting a Sauvignon from New Zealand and another from the Loire (blind) with a fish dish. The chances are that they will respond to food in very different ways.**

CLOUDY BAY

One of the earliest ambassadors of the style was a wine called Cloudy Bay that first appeared on the lists of swanky restaurants in the late '80s. Initially, it was a curiosity—"The New Zealanders make wine, do they? Now there's a thing. Have another glass." Soon it was not because of novelty that corporate lunchers were crying out for more, but because of the wine's fabulous combination of zingy freshness and a delightful herbaceous character that made Loire whites such as Pouilly Fumé and Sancerre pale into insignificance. Though the success of New Zealand wine on the export market can hardly be attributed to one wine, Cloudy Bay's success did put the country on the map in the way that no advertising campaign could have hoped to. Perhaps one of the best aspects of its success was that Cloudy Bay—unlike Jacob's Creek, Australia's ambassador on the world stage—wasn't cheap. It was comparable in price to the swanky Loire whites—but far, far better. The rest is history.

Over the last decade or so, new grapes and styles have proliferated. But what has been the secret of New Zealand's success? A key factor has been climate. You only need to look at photographs of the lush, misty landscape of areas such as Marlborough, New Zealand's most successful winemaking region, to realize that such a country offers the perfect conditions for crisp, cool-climate wines of the kind previously associated with areas such as the Loire, Burgundy, Germany, and Alsace. In addition, the country's wines have benefited from the same advantages as those in Australia, Chile, and South Africa—namely straightforward labels that consumers can understand. It is little wonder that producers in Europe's classic wine regions have been woken up from their complacency.

TASTE TEST

- Good-quality New Zealand Sauvignon Blanc
- New Zealand Riesling
- New Zealand Pinot Gris
- Sancerre or Pouilly Fumé
- Pinot Grigio
- Dry-style German Riesling
- Burgundian Pinot Noir

First carry out random comparisons before trying out the following combinations:

- New Zealand Sauvignon Blanc + Pouilly Fumé or Sancerre
- New Zealand Riesling + dry-style German Riesling
- New Zealand Pinot Gris + Pinot Grigio
- New Zealand Pinot Noir + Burgundian Pinot Noir

COMPARE AND CONTRAST

If you detected a difference in style between the wines in the taste test this is a good time to think about the variety of approaches to winemaking in different wine regions. There is a tendency among New World winemakers—particularly those in New Zealand—to extract every last drop of flavor from a grape, whereas those in Europe tend to go for wines with a little more subtlety. This is a charitable view—those who champion the cause of New World winemakers might say that their in-your-face wines are simply the result of superior winemaking skills.

If you like the in-your-face style of New Zealand whites try some other whites with attitude in IDEA 9, *Whites with attitude.*

Try another idea...

"I think it's fair to say that New Zealand Sauvignon Blanc changed the wine world by changing our ideas of what wine could be like."
OZ CLARKE

Defining idea...

115

How did
it go?

Q   I noticed that both the whites and the reds from New Zealand were much more aromatic than most of their European counterparts. Why is this?

A   *It is really the result of a combination of climate and winemaking. It's also a matter of style. New World winemaking tends to be more about extracting every last drop of flavor from a grape, whereas in Europe there's a taste for a more subtle, more discreet style of wine. The more you taste, the sooner you will develop a preference for one of these two divergent styles.*

Q   I have also found that the New Zealand wines often overpower food. What would you say to that?

A   *It is something that you need to bear in mind. Though the more restrained style of Loire Sauvignon is well suited to summery dishes with subtle flavors (asparagus being the obvious example), punchy New Zealand Sauvignon might need something with a spicier edge.*

Q   Although there were similarities between some of the white wines, I found that the New Zealand Pinot Noir had very little in common with the Burgundian equivalent. Why is that?

A   *It's because of the notoriously fickle nature of the Pinot Noir grape. Pinot Noir creates a greater number of styles than almost any other variety—a fact that makes it the object of much fascination among winemakers. In some climates it will make delicate, bony styles, whereas in others it can create much more approachable, raspberry-ish wines.*

28

California dreaming

The vineyards near the West Coast are among the most beautiful in the world. Yet does the relentless pursuit of technical perfection in Californian wineries create wines that are the stuff of dreams or are they a little bland?

Anyone who has ever driven north across the Golden Gate through Napa, Sonoma, and Mendocino will tell you that California's wine country is God's own country.

Its sweeping, perfectly formed terrain, lush vineyards, and exquisite cuisine wineries with welcoming visitor centers make California an ideal place to learn about wine. Few places could be further removed from the disheveled vines and locked gates that meet visitors to so many European wine-producing regions.

Not only are California's vineyards fabulously well groomed, so are its wines. There are those who argue that many Californian wines are textbook examples of the winemaker's art. The region's critics believe that great winemakers don't need textbooks, that perfect wines are bland and lacking in character. It won't be until you have drunk your way around the Californian wines that you will be able to take

If there is a wine region where the obsession with winemaking reaches almost maniacal intensity it is California, where they see matching food and wine as a sort of alchemy that relies on a precise marriage of complementary flavors. As food and wine matching is such an intrinsic part of the region's gastronomic heritage, it makes sense to match Californian wines with food, preferably with sunny Californian-style food.

a view, so until then keep an open mind. Like any wine region, California evades generalizations. As you will discover, it's the home of good and boring wines in equal measure.

One problem that has blighted the Californian wine industry in recent years has been competition. Until recently, the region's winemakers had a near monopoly over the market for non-European wines in the United States. However, the recent arrival of good-value wines from Chile and Australia has generated fierce competition. Another fly in the ointment has been oversupply. The exponential growth in the number of wineries has created such a serious glut that Californian producers have had to drop prices in order to remain competitive. The result is excellent news for drinkers: oversupply means good-value wines—in many cases, superb examples of their type.

TASTE TEST—WHITES

- Californian Chardonnay
- Australian Chardonnay
- Good Californian sparkling wine
- Good Champagne
- Australian sparkling wine

TASTE TEST—REDS

- Californian Cabernet
- Australian Cabernet
- Red Bordeaux
- Californian Zinfandel
- Californian Pinot Noir
- Good-quality Burgundy
- Australian Cabernet Sauvignon
- Good-quality Cabernet-based red Bordeaux
- Rhône red

COMPARE AND CONTRAST

Having tried the wines blind, try the following lineup:
- Californian Chardonnay + Australian Chardonnay
- Californian Cabernet + Australian Cabernet + Cabernet-based red Bordeaux
- Californian Zinfandel + Rhône red + Californian Cabernet
- Californian Pinot Noir + good-quality Burgundy
- Good Californian sparkling wine + good Champagne + Australian sparkling wine

Other than Chardonnay, California's great speciality is Cabernet. For more on this versatile grape see IDEA 20, *Counting on Cabernet.*

Try another idea...

"The great majority of those who speak of perfectibility as a dream do so because they feel that it is one which would afford them no pleasure if it is realized."
JOHN STUART MILL

Defining idea...

119

ALL YOU NEED TO KNOW ABOUT ZINFANDEL

Almost every wine region has a grape or grapes that it has made its own. Burgundy has Chardonnay and Burgundy. The Loire has Sauvignon Blanc. Australia has Shiraz. South Africa has Pinotage. California's speciality is Zinfandel, a grape of obscure origins that makes wonderfully bold reds and terrible rosé known as "blush."

A SHORT HISTORY OF CALIFORNIAN WINE

Vines have been grown in the region since the 1770s, but it wasn't until the gold rush in the 1850s that an influx of thirsty prospectors created a market for locally produced wines. In the late nineteenth century and the early twentieth the double whammy of phylloxera—a devastating disease that destroys vines—and prohibition gave the industry a bumpy ride. Things improved after World War II, although the market—like that in Australia—was still for sweet wines. In the '60s a new generation of dry table wines, notably Cabernet Sauvignon and Chardonnay, gained serious recognition, notably at a landmark tasting in 1976 when some Californian reds beat some of Bordeaux's top chateaux in a blind tasting.

Q **Isn't it a good thing when winemakers strive for perfection?**

How did it go?

A *It really depends on what sort of wines you like. Some people like wonderfully poised whites and smooth, glossy reds. Others feel that an imperfection or two adds character. It's like the difference between a brand-new, gleaming piece of furniture and one that has begun to show signs of age. It is really just a matter of personal taste.*

Q **What sort of food should Zinfandel be drunk with?**

A *There are no rules to matching food and wine. But as a start, why not try Zinfandel with a hearty casserole or some strongly flavored charcuterie?*

Q **I was surprised to discover that some Champagne houses and Bordeaux chateaux also make wine in California. Doesn't that undermine their argument that Champagne is the best region in the world in which to make sparkling wine?**

A *You'd have thought so, but they have been quite astute in keeping the Californian brands distinct. If anything, they support the idea that California can't quite compete with Europe for character and finesse.*

29

The Italian renaissance

In the '80s the Italians churned out some pretty ordinary wine—and we drank it in huge quantities. But twenty years later these producers have learned their lesson and are producing wines that offer light relief from the predictable flavors of Aussie Chardonnay.

Every leisure pursuit from birdwatching to rappeling has its fair share of hardened nutcases who love nothing more than a tortuous challenge.

Wine appreciation is no exception—and there are few wine-producing regions to which hard-core enthusiasts are more obsessively attracted than Italy. In the same way that vintage car enthusiasts love the unpredictability of old engines, so fans of Italian wine love the quirks and eccentricities to be found in the character reds and quirky whites of Tuscany, Piedmont, the Veneto, Basilicata, and Sicily. They seem to find the predictable flavors and consistent quality of New World wines so mind-numbing that they prefer to go in search of a bit of danger among the wild, wonderful, and in some cases, ruinously expensive wines that Italy offers. There is no doubt, either, that many people are attracted by the romance of Italian wine—the exquisite castelli, sweeping vineyards, crumbling wineries, and fabulous food proving the theory that wine drinkers are better disposed toward wine regions where they would actually like to be.

Here's an idea for you...

Italians see wine as part of their culture. However corny it might sound, it always helps to create the right environment in which to enjoy Italian wine— with the help of some prosciutto, bread, olive oil. Yes, and some Verdi . . .

But like all European wine-producing countries, Italy has taken a knock in recent decades. While in the '70s and '80s we were happy to quaff indifferent Chianti, Soave, Pinot Grigio, and Frascati with our lasagne al forno, the arrival of more flavorsome, fruitier wines from Australia and Chile spelled the end of the heyday of cheap and cheerful Italian wine.

Since then, two things have happened. The first is that mass-market producers have realized that they must clean up their act and either set out to improve the quality of their wines or try to emulate the success of the New World by producing fruity, good-value Chardonnays, Sauvignons, Merlots, and Cabernets. The second is that at a higher level a new generation of smaller producers, particularly in areas such as Piedmont and Tuscany, have concentrated their efforts on creating fabulous—and fabulously expensive—wines that age beautifully.

The bad news is that Italy now provides a more complex minefield for drinkers than ever before, with the result that it demands more radical weeding through than almost any other wine region.

TASTE TEST—REDS

- Barolo
- Good-quality Chianti
- Inexpensive Chianti
- Salice Salentino
- Expensive Australian or Chilean Cabernet

To help your palate feel its way around the different flavors, compare these wines side by side so that you get a feel for the profile of the different flavors and aromas offered by each of them.

TASTE TEST—WHITES

- Soave
- Frascati
- Orvieto
- Sicilian Chardonnay
- Verdicchio dei Castelli di Jesi

COMPARE AND CONTRAST

With a few exceptions these are wines—like those from France and Spain—in which style and region take precedence over the grape variety. Chianti, for example, is made from a blend that includes a grape called Sangiovese that is indigenous to Italy, Soave is made from Garganega and Trebbiano grapes, and Barolo from Nebbiolo. But how much do their contents matter, particularly since many of these wines contain blends of more than one grape and are made by people who care more about wine that reflects its origins than its grapes?

Conspicuous by its absence in the taste test was Prosecco, the wonderful sparkling wine from northern Italy. You'll find it in another taste test in IDEA 23, _Lovely bubbly?_, which compares Prosecco with other sparkling wines.

Try another idea...

"Enthusiasts for Italian wine have never had such an embarrassment of riches."
THE OXFORD COMPANION TO WINE

Defining idea...

125

Tasting Italian wines also requires a particular mind-set. As in many countries where wine is ingrained into the national gastronomic culture, wine is an integral part of a meal but not the main attraction. Anyone used to the big, attention-grabbing flavors of New World wines will find the more shy and retiring nature of wines such as Soave and Frascati hard to fathom. Imagine drinking them with a spaghetti carbonara on a boiling hot afternoon in Tuscany and their appeal suddenly becomes more apparent.

How did it go?

Q   You were right. I found some of the whites a bit limp compared with what I am used to. Any tips?

A   *Yes, stick with them. Food isn't the only thing that has a bearing on our enjoyment of Italian wine. So does the occasion. Try drinking a glass of ice cold Italian Frascati on a hot day and you will see it in a new light.*

Q   I found the Barolo extraordinary and rather overpowering. Should I assume that it is intended to be drunk with food?

A   *It's not called the "King of Wines and the Wine of Kings" for nothing. Try it with a rich hare or beef casserole.*

Q   You mention that some Italian producers are creating "New World" Chardonnays and Merlots. Are they any good?

A   *They're fine but they won't help you understand the true character of Italian wine—they could have been made anywhere.*

30
Sherry baby

A sickly old-fashioned drink fit only for the drain, or one of the world's best-value and underrated wines? Focus on the best examples and you might soon have an opinion.

For as long as anyone can remember, a succession of PR companies acting on behalf of the Sherry industry have been predicting that Sherry is on the cusp of becoming the fashionable drink of thirty-something drinkers.

The theory of the spin-meisters is this: For years Sherry's reputation was damaged by disgustingly sweet cloying styles favored by aged aunts. Now, however, a new generation of drinkers is about to discover the joys of keeping a chilled bottle of Fino in the fridge to provide a great alternative to white wine or gin and tonic when aperitifs are called for. The more optimistic of the PR people predicted that the growing popularity of Spanish food—notably tapas—would encourage drinkers to consume Sherry throughout a meal. Dream on. The fact that such spin seems to ignore is that wine isn't about fashion: most people drink whatever suits their tastes and their pocket.

Here's an idea for you... **Do what the PR people have been willing you to do for a decade. Keep a bottle of Sherry in the fridge for use as an early evening sharpener. One evening you could even make the PR dream come true by drinking it as an accompaniment to food. (Remember that it has quite a high alcohol content.)**

The reason for the huge success of Sherry during the '50s and '60s was that it was an inexpensive, potent, and supposedly long-lived alternative to wine. But now that wine is cheaper we think nothing of cracking open a bottle at the drop of a hat.

There is only one fact that any PR person needs to convince the public about, namely that Fino Sherry is arguably the most delicious, best-value, highest-quality wine known to humankind. It sounds like a bold claim, doesn't it? So in order to decide where you stand on the issue you need to undertake a most dramatic exercise in weeding out.

Imagine that you woke up in a world where there was no Manzanilla, no Manzanilla Pasada, no Cream Sherry, no Pale Sherry, no Palo Cortado, no Amontillado, no Oloroso, and where Pedro Ximenez was not a dark style of sweet Sherry but a Spanish bullfighter. Imagine that the only style of Sherry in existence is Fino.

It sounds radical, doesn't it? But like all previous suggestions, the idea is not that you never allow any other type of Sherry to pass your lips, but simply that if you are to learn to understand Fino you must renounce all other Sherries. At this stage it is an essential step on your path to vinous nirvana.

SHERRY AND FOOD

Because it is fortified (i.e., had alcohol added to it), many people believe that Sherry should only be drunk as an aperitif. However, it makes an excellent partner to food—in Andalucia, where it is made, it is not uncommon to see diners drinking Sherry throughout a meal. Sherry has an affinity with the same dishes that go well with dry whites, such as fish and seafood. However, if you are drinking it as an aperitif, the best accompaniment is toasted almonds.

To put Sherry into the context of the country it comes from, turn to IDEA 24, *Spanish highs*, for more on Spanish wines in general.

Try another idea...

TASTE TEST

- Good-quality Fino
- Cheap Fino
- Cheap Port
- Pouilly Fume
- White Rioja
- Cheap Australian Chardonnay

"One does not think of Sherry normally in direct comparison with the other great white wines of the world—but it is, strange to say, the cheapest of them."
HUGH JOHNSON

Defining idea...

COMPARE AND CONTRAST

Tasting these wines side by side will help you to put the unique character of Fino into context. The point to remember when tasting these wines is that Fino is fortified to a strength of around 15 percent—double that of some light German wines and a third more than most white wines. On an empty stomach you'll find that it packs an even more powerful punch.

EVERYTHING YOU NEED TO KNOW ABOUT FINO

1. It is made in Andalucia near the seaside towns of Jerez de la Frontera ("Jerez" is the origin of the English name "Sherry"), Sanlucar de Barrameda, and Puerto de Santa Maria.
2. It is made from a white grape called Palomino Fino, which makes pretty dull table wines but great Fino Sherry thanks to a natural yeast called "flor" that is created by the Sherry-making process. The flor forms a mushy layer that sits on the top of Sherry as it is aged.
3. Fino is created by a curious, complex process known as the solera system in which, after a few years in the barrel, a third of the oldest Sherry is bottled and the remainder is topped up with younger Sherry before being aged further.

How did it go?

Q **Some of the Finos I have tasted had an almost salty character. Why is this?**

A *That is one of the characteristics of Fino. There is a fanciful belief that Fino and its close cousin, Manzanilla, derive their saltiness from the fact that they are made so close to the sea.*

Q **Some people keep Sherry in decanters for months. Is this a good idea?**

A *No. Sherry should be kept—airtight—in a fridge and consumed within a few days. Once you get a taste for it, you'll be consuming it in a few hours.*

Q **Any suggestions for drinking Sherry in a gastronomic context?**

A *Tapas are the obvious accompaniment—but nothing beats salted almonds.*

31

Que Syrah, Syrah

Syrah—the classic red grape of the Rhône Valley—has been reinvented by Australian winemakers with such success that they have given birth to a style of wine that is all their own. They have even given it their own name.

Of all the well-known red grape varieties, Cabernet might be the ubiquitous crowd pleaser but Syrah is the variety that has succeeded in beguiling winemakers all over the world from the Rhone Valley—its spiritual home—to Australia's Barossa region.

Before we go any further, let's clear up a few confusing Syrah-related minutiae.

ALL YOU NEED TO KNOW ABOUT SYRAH

■ In the Rhône, where Syrah is used to make legendary long-lived red wines such as Hermitage, the grape is known as "Syrah."

Here's an
idea for
you... **The Rhône is another wine region that needs a map. Start putting all the famous names such as Hermitage and Chateauneuf du Pape into context by plotting their origin.**

- In Australia, where Syrah has been grown since the early nineteenth century—as well as in South Africa, where it has also been embraced with much enthusiasm—the grape is known as "Shiraz."

- As you will discover, the difference isn't just one of name: In different climates Syrah/Shiraz is used to produce two entirely different styles of wine.

So, although this Idea is devoted to both manifestations of the grape, Shiraz and Syrah could almost be considered as two different varieties. In the Rhône, Syrah is either used on its own or blended with a variety of other reds such as Cinsault, Carignan, and Mourverdre. In the New World, particularly in Australia, the grape is used on its own or sometimes blended with Cabernet.

TASTE TEST

The difference between Shiraz and Syrah will become clear in the following taste test:

- Red Hermitage or Crozes Hermitage (entirely Syrah-based)
- Rhône red made from a blend of grapes including Syrah
- Inexpensive Australian Shiraz
- Expensive Barossa Shiraz
- South African Shiraz
- Good-quality Australian Cabernet

COMPARE AND CONTRAST

Compare these wines side by side and you should get an idea of the varying character of the grape. How do those produced in the hotter climate of Australia compare with those produced in the Rhône? Are there any differences between the South African and the Australian Shiraz?

You'll have a better understanding of Shiraz when you know more about its spiritual homeland–the Rhône. For more on this fascinating region turn to IDEA 43, *A river runs through it.*

Try another idea...

A SHORT HISTORY OF SYRAH

There are various theories about the origins of the grape. One is that it was brought to the Rhône from ancient Persia in the saddlebags of returning crusaders. Another is that it is indigenous and has been used to make wine in the area since Roman times. Of all its different Rhône guises, the most legendary is Hermitage, the ruinously expensive, long-lived wine admired by the wine-loving Thomas Jefferson, as well as by the Russian imperial court.

"Sometimes Shiraz has all the subtlety of an oversexed bus."
BRUCE TYRRELL

Defining idea...

133

A SHORT HISTORY OF SHIRAZ

The grape is thought to have been exported to Australia by James Busby, the father of Australian viticulture. A century later it gained a legendary reputation as Grange, a fabulously complex red made in the Barossa by Max Schubert, the chief winemaker at Penfolds. The wine, which doesn't show its best qualities until after a decade or so, is widely acknowledged as one of Australia's greatest wines and proved to sniffy Europeans that Australian winemakers could make serious wine. The grape is now almost as widely planted in the country as Chardonnay.

THE "FOOD WINE" EUPHEMISM

Australian Shiraz is one of those wines often described as a "food wine." The term is a euphemism for a wine that would taste much too overpowering on its own and needs to be tempered by the soothing effects of food. However, the more examples of the wine you taste, the more you will comprehend the variation in styles from restrained and peppery to big and overblown. Remember, too, that wines such as Syrah are not intended to be drunk on their own. A light, chilled red might make a good alternative to white wine on a warm summer evening but heavy reds were never intended as aperitifs. This is one of the reasons that wines can be rather misrepresented by being tasted in the clinical environment of a tasting room. Bear this in mind when you are tasting all heavy reds—and ideally have some food on hand to put them into context.

Q **Why do the same grapes from two different parts of the world, the Rhône and Australia, taste so different?**

A *It's more about weather than winemaking.*

Q **Why is it that, when compared with Cabernet, Syrah and Shiraz seem much bolder and in-your-face?**

A *The grape makes wines that tend to be a lot richer than Cabernet. But the effect you've noticed might not just be caused by the grape; it could also arise from the wine having too much oak.*

Q **You describe Shiraz as a "food wine." What sort of food should particularly bold Shiraz be served with?**

A *Try food with sufficiently big and bold flavors to survive the onslaught. Big hearty stews would be perfect. Just avoid anything that's too subtle.*

How did it go?

32

The merchants of menace

A good wine merchant is as essential as a bottle opener. Not only are the best hugely knowledgeable, they also sell wines that you are unlikely to find elsewhere.

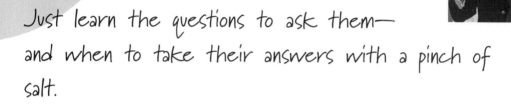

Just learn the questions to ask them—
and when to take their answers with a pinch of
salt.

Let's start by tackling two caricatures of the wine merchant that often inhibit people's use of them.

THE SNOB

Suave, suited, and slightly patronizing, old school wine merchants are really interested in one thing: France. The names of the famous estates fall off their tongues effortlessly: Echezeaux, Domaine de la Romanee Conti, Yquem. They love the romance of wine: the chateaux, the terroir, the damp old cellars. In their drinking they rarely stray much beyond Bordeaux, Burgundy, and the Loire— although they make the occasional foray into Mosel for crisp, refreshing whites and, of course, to Portugal for after-dinner vintage Port. Their natural reticence doesn't make them obvious salespeople and they assume a great deal of knowledge—a fact that makes non-wine-buffs regard them as completely terrifying.

Here's an idea for you...

Visit all the specialist wine outlets in your area and try to identify one that has a staff member in whom you have confidence by asking a few questions and trying out his or her recommendations. An ongoing relationship is more fruitful than occasional encounters, since you will begin to understand one another's likes and dislikes.

THE NERD

Nerdy wine merchants could have turned their obsessive curiosity to anything—computers, ornithology, old tractors—but by some twist of fate it happened to be wine. Wine for nerds is not about pleasure; it's about malolactic fermentation, yeasty autolysis, and vintage variation. They are interested in anything that carries the name "wine"—dusty old bottles of Romanian Pinot Noir, Uruguayan Tannat, Canadian Eiswein—but their real love is New World winemaking, largely because they regard winemakers in Australia, New Zealand, and South Africa as more relaxed and less snobby. Behind a counter they are helpful, but their speech is so loaded with jargon and detail that they tend to leave their customers feeling utterly confused.

The problem faced by the free-thinking drinker is that there is quite a lot of truth in both stereotypes. However much the wine trade believes that they have "democratized" wine in the last decade or so, both the snobs and the nerds continue to dominate the scene; the snobs giving the impression that wine appreciation is an elite pursuit and the nerds blinding their customers with science. Nevertheless, the joy of wine merchants is that they are knowledgeable enthusiasts who love their subject.

THE SECRET OF SPOTTING A GOOD WINE MERCHANT

Look for the following signs:
- They offer you a chance to try wines.
- They don't sell cigarettes and sweets by the register.
- They sell specialist wine magazines, fancy corkscrews, and wineglasses.

A good wine merchant should fulfill a similar role to that of a sommelier—although it sometimes makes sense to give the latter more leeway. See **IDEA 25, *A user's guide to sommeliers.***

Try another idea...

In order to use a wine merchant successfully you need a tactical, focused approach. Asking a wine merchant for "a decent red/white to take to a dinner party" is as much of a leap of faith as asking a sales assistant in a department store to choose you an outfit without you trying it on.

What is essential is to be specific and to set parameters, particularly when looking for wines to be used in a taste test. A better bet would be "Could I have a good-value New Zealand Sauvignon Blanc?" or "Do you have a good-quality, typical Sancerre?" The secret is not to allow yourself to be led down some other route that a wine merchant wants you to take.

A SOURCE OF ADVICE

A wine merchant can be a good source of advice—but remember that the key to achieving vinous nirvana is not to let yourself become a receptacle for other people's opinions. Also remember that wine merchants

"Knowledge dwells in heads replete with thoughts of other men; wisdom in minds attentive to their own."
WILLIAM COWPER

Defining idea...

139

are not just wine enthusiasts; they are also salespeople. So beware: They might have a reason to sell you one wine rather than another—such as the fact that it has a higher profit margin or it needs to be shifted. Nevertheless, handled carefully, merchants can be guides who will offer essential advice to the free-thinking drinker.

A SOURCE OF UNUSUAL WINES?

This is where wine merchants really come into their own. Although supermarkets are undoubtedly a great source of good-value branded wines, their buying departments have an approach to wine that is very different from that of a wine merchant. Their wine, like anything else on the supermarket shelves, is more a matter of profit margins than quality. On the whole, supermarkets favor fast-selling wines that are supplied in large quantities rather than offbeat wines that don't make a quick, profitable return. Though wine merchants also need to make a profit from their wines, they are aware that their raison d'être is to offer greater choice to a more discerning audience.

MAINTAINING YOUR INDEPENDENCE

For the free-thinking drinker, one of the dangers of a wine merchant is that you might fall too much under their influence. Question everything they tell you. If you like wines they have recommended, tell them.

Q **Why is it more important to be specific when dealing with a wine merchant than with a sommelier?**

How did it go?

A *Because in order to deepen your understanding of wine you need to compare specific wines. Restaurant wine lists should be used as an opportunity to discover new styles of wine.*

Q **Isn't wine much cheaper elsewhere?**

A *Mass-market wines usually are. But that isn't what specialist wine merchants are about; they are about providing choice and guidance.*

Q **Isn't it much less convenient to make trips to specialist merchants?**

A *Yes, but it's worth the effort. Besides, once you have established a relationship you can start doing business over the phone or Internet.*

33

The secret of a happy marriage

The art of matching food and wine has spawned countless rules and regulations dreamed up by obsessive foodies. However, the key to a sensual, satisfying relationship is an open mind.

If you think that wine has among its enormous following more than its fair share of bores, pedants, and nitpickers, then consider the related field of food and wine matching.

Food and wine matching is an obsession to which most of its protagonists graduate once they have explored every possible aspect of wine—mastered every conceivable grape variety, familiarized themselves with every wine region and every intimate detail of the winemaking process—so that now they feel it is time to scale a new mountain: the huge, fabulously subjective business of which wines go best with which food.

Here's an idea for you...

Always try to keep two to three bottles of wine open at any given time. The more combinations you try, the greater chance you'll have of finding a good match.

THE OBSESSIVE APPROACH

The fervently held belief of the obsessives is that every food has its natural, preordained bedfellow: Wood pigeon with St. Emilion, chargrilled asparagus with Pouilly Fume, syllabub with Sauternes, and so on. The theory is that there are flavors to be found in various foods and wines that, when combined, are transformed by some gastronomic alchemy to create a taste sensation that makes sexual pleasure pale into insignificance.

THE PATH OF MODERATION

The moderates believe that food and wine are both integral parts of the gastronomic experience but, however symbiotic the relationship, they don't lose any sleep over the subject. They simply believe that it is great when it works and fine when it doesn't.

THE ANARCHIST CREED

This theory is that anything goes with anything. If it tastes good, do it.

The only way to discover where you stand on food and wine matching is to experiment. But in the same way that it is essential to avoid becoming a receptacle of other people's opinions on wine, it is also essential that you follow your own instincts when exploring which food goes well with which wine.

TASTE TEST

Try the following combinations:
- Hot spicy lamb curry + New Zealand Sauvignon Blanc + Australian Shiraz
- Chicken in tarragon sauce + New Zealand Sauvignon Blanc + Australian Shiraz + oaky Australian Chardonnay

A good source of inspiration on food and wine matching is a sommelier. See IDEA 25, *A user's guide to sommeliers.*

Try another idea...

COMPARE AND CONTRAST

How did the flavors of the wines respond to the different types of food, and vice versa? The secret of a successful wine match is similar to that of a successful wine— you are offered flavors that balance one another beautifully.

When you start investigating wine in the context of food and food in the context of wine, you're pulling the lid off a vast arena of gastronomy. What won't help your understanding is to ask the question "Why?" Obsessives love dreaming up theories about why certain wines do or don't go with certain types of food, in order to make certain hard and fast rules (almost every wine handbook has one of these lurking toward the back). But matching food and wine is not a subject that can be easily regulated. For years there was a fervently held belief that cheese should only ever be eaten with red wines and sweet wines until one esteemed wine expert was brave enough to stick his hand up and say he felt that soft,

"Red with meat, white with fish, except lox or herring. Rosé with any endangered species or an ice cream cone."
RICHARD SMITH, *A Gentleman's Guide to Wines*

Defining idea...

Defining
idea...

"I often wonder whether those who so vehemently proscribe certain wine and food combinations do so from unhappy experience or from untested acceptance of rules. Just a few years ago we raised our glasses (unknowingly filled with 1923 Rayne-Vigneau Sauternes), there was a delighted murmur from each of us at this quite unexpected taste sensation produced by this dry-sweet old wine–rich in flavors rather than sugars–in combination with the delicate richness of the fish. What rule would have told me to drink fine old Sauternes with smoked salmon?"
GERALD ASHER

creamy cheeses with delicate flavors were far better suited to white wines rather than reds.

THE REGIONAL APPROACH

One sensible approach to the business of food and wine matching is to try—whenever possible—to combine food that is typical of a region with its wines, e.g., red Burgundy with boeuf bourguignon, Swiss whites with fondue, Moroccan reds with tagine.

THE ONLY GOLDEN RULE . . .

. . . doesn't dictate which wine you should drink with which food but says that you should treat wine as an intrinsic part of the gastronomic experience. Wine doesn't exist to be tasted in the clinical environment of a tasting room with nothing more than a dry cracker for company. Almost all wine (however bad) tastes better with food than without it.

Q   Should wine never be drunk without food?

A   If you are drinking a wine in order to stimulate your appetite, it doesn't necessarily make sense to accompany it with food.

Q   Surely rules are a useful guideline?

A   Because everyone has different tastes it is almost impossible to generalize about successful food and wine matches. If you insist on following rules, make sure that you are prepared to break them.

Q   Why is wine so difficult to match with curry?

A   Because the flavors of many spices combine with those in wine to create a rather unattractive taste in the mouth. There are many who believe that the best accompaniment to curry is either beer or lassi, a yogurt-based drink popular in India.

How did it go?

147

34

Money talks

The fact that a perfectly decent bottle of wine costs very little while a slightly better one can cost a hundred times more begs the question of whether there's any real correlation between price and flavor.

The joy of being a free-thinking drinker is that you'll be able to spot a rip-off wine at fifty paces.

In countries where wine is considered an unnecessary luxury rather than an everyday commodity, wine appreciation tends to be inextricably linked with that most dreary of subjects—its cost. But what compounds our feelings of guilt about spending money on wine is confusion. Wine is rather like contemporary art: no one is really sure of its true worth. In the same way that we are confused by the fact that one conceptual daub might be worth hundreds or thousands of times more than another, many of us can't really fathom the reason that the price of a bottle of wine can vary so dramatically—particularly since the price of a decent bottle is now relatively much lower than it was a decade or so ago. Much of the problem is that the pricing of wine isn't as transparent as, say, the cost of a car. When you look at the price of a family van, for example, it is completely apparent why one model is more expensive than another. When you look at a wine list the reason that one wine is twice the price of another is far from obvious.

Here's an
idea for
you... **When conducting taste tests
try to guess the approximate
price of the wine in your glass.
Doing so will focus your
mind on the correlation between
price and quality—or, indeed,
the lack of it.**

TASTE TEST

This test is one that you should try when there are at least half a dozen tasters around:

- Prosecco + Cava + good-quality New World sparkling wine + well-known Champagne brand

Give each of the tasters a sheet with a list of the prices and ask them to try to match them with the wines. Look at the disparities in the responses and ask yourself whether the same tasters would have had the same problem if you had asked them to match four different cars with their price tags.

WHY SOME WINES ARE CHEAP

- They are made in countries where land and labor are cheap, e.g., South America and Eastern Europe.
- They are made from grapes grown in hot regions where vines are irrigated in order to produce a large quantity of fruit that lacks flavor—a problem solved in the winery by the use of additives such as oak chips.
- They are made in an area where there happens to be huge over-supply.
- They are made by large producers able to take advantage of economies of scale.
- They are on sale—usually an occasional discount that is almost always funded by desperate producers in order to secure a permanent listing with a retailer.
- They don't taste very nice.

WHY SOME WINES ARE EXPENSIVE

- They are made in countries where land and labor are expensive.
- They come from a region or producer that has traditionally been held in high esteem, e.g., Bordeaux, Burgundy, and Champagne.
- They are made from a particularly good vintage (a point most relevant to Bordeaux, Burgundy, and Champagne).
- They are painstakingly made by small specialist producers that are unable to take advantage of economies of scale.
- They are promoted with expensive marketing campaigns.
- They taste delicious.

As you can see, there are plenty of reasons why wines can be cheap or expensive that don't necessarily have anything to do with their quality. It is because wine is such a subjective field—and so many wine drinkers lack confidence in their opinions—that some producers are able to charge high prices for very ordinary wines. The result is that wines produced in regions where land and labor are expensive have to do a great deal to convince the world that they have some sort of divinely ordained mystique.

Try another idea...

The success with which wine producers in Bordeaux, Burgundy, and Champagne have convinced the world that their wines are worth paying inflated prices for is explored further in IDEA 21, *Bordeaux, Burgundy, and Champagne.*

Defining idea...

"A man who is rich in adolescence is almost doomed to be a dilettante at table. This is not because all millionaires are stupid but because they are not compelled to experiment."
A. J. LIEBLING

How did it go?

Q **In the taste test there didn't appear to be much correlation between the tasters' scores and the prices. Is this the fault of the wines or the tasters?**

A   *The wines.*

Q **Are you saying that a cheap wine made in a region with little prestige where overheads are low and output is high, and sold to a supermarket at a discount, could be just as delicious as a more expensive wine made by a high-profile producer in a prestigious region where overheads are high and output is low?**

A   *It could be. The only way to judge it is with your taste buds.*

Q **Why do people tend to be more concerned about price in countries where there isn't much tradition of winemaking?**

A   *Partly because of high taxation and also because they regard it as an unnecessary luxury. In countries such as France or Italy wine is simply seen as part of everyday life.*

35

On doctor's orders?

The wine industry might try to promote wine as an intrinsic part of a healthy diet, but there is no doubt that the effects of heavy drinking are calamitous. Learn to distinguish the myths from the realities.

Read as much as you like about the subject of wine and health and you won't come across many conclusive opinions.

On an almost weekly basis some new study is published promoting the benefits of wine consumption and is contradicted by another blaming wine for a catalog of ills.

THE GRIM TRUTH

However much the pro-wine lobby might champion the cause of wine consumption, wine is known to be linked to liver damage, brain damage, cancer, nerve and muscle wasting, blood disorders, raised blood pressure, strokes, skin infections, psoriasis, infertility, and birth defects. Wine consumption can also be blamed for all sorts of collateral damage such as road accidents and domestic violence.

Here's an idea for you... **Try to follow the French habit of only ever drinking wine with a meal. Not only does wine taste better with food, it also means that once the wine has been consumed there is sufficient food to absorb some of it in the stomach (try drinking on an empty stomach and you will get the idea). Also have plenty of water an hand. It never pays to quench your thirst with wine.**

Defining idea... *"The cheapness of wine seems to be a cause, not of drunkenness but of sobriety . . . People are seldom guilty of excess in what is their daily fare . . . On the contrary, in the countries which either from excessive heat or cold produce no grapes, and where wine consequently is dear and a rarity, drunkenness is a common vice."*
ADAM SMITH

SOBERING, ISN'T IT?

One fact that undermines the case of the pro-wine lobby is that much of the research is sponsored by those who have a vested interest in the continued growth of wine consumption. Yet, aside from the rash claims made by studies published by various universities (many of which happen to be located in winemaking regions such as Bordeaux and Burgundy), there is fairly convincing evidence that moderate wine consumption does have some benefits. Drinking between one and three glasses of wine a day is believed to reduce the chances of cardiovascular disease. Despite technically being toxic, alcohol offers such benefits as controlling the levels of blood cholesterol and blood-clotting proteins.

One of the great planks of the wine–health debate is based on what is known as the "French paradox"—the discovery made by US documentary makers that, despite a relatively high intake of alcohol, the French were generally much healthier than people in Anglo-Saxon countries where drinking is more moderate. If this true, then one of the contributory factors—besides the

"Mediterranean diet" high in fresh fruit and olive oil—might be the rate at which alcohol is consumed. The tendency in many other parts of the world is to binge, i.e., to concentrate drinking into a relatively short period of time. In France, since wine is an intrinsic part of the gastronomic experience, the rule seems to be "a little but often."

There is also an argument that those who see wines as a source of sensual pleasure are likely to drink less wine than those who drink simply to get drunk. The more that free-thinking drinkers immerse themselves in the field of wine appreciation by learning to savor the wonderful flavors and aromas that wine offers, the less they will see wine as a social prop.

THE PROBLEM OF CHEAP WINE

A growing problem in recent years that is rarely highlighted is the falling price of wine; the combination of better technology and increased volume of wine being produced has meant that the cost of a bottle has fallen dramatically over the last twenty years. The fact that wine is no longer a luxury and is so much more accessible has helped to drive up wine consumption.

Try another idea...

It is important to see wine as an intrinsic part of the gastronomic experience. If you make a habit of drinking good-quality, interesting wines well suited to the food you are eating with them, you are much less likely to binge. There's more on food and wine matching in IDEA 33, *The secret of a happy marriage.*

Defining idea...

"*Fermented beverages have been preferred over water throughout the ages: they are safer, provide psychotropic effects, and are more nutritious. Some have even said that alcohol was the primary agent for the development of Western civilization, since more healthy individuals (even if inebriated for much of the time) lived longer and had greater reproductive success.*"
PATRICK McGOVERN

There is no doubt, too, that cheap wine now tastes much better than it ever did in the past—leaps and bounds in winemaking know-how have created a new generation of fruity, inexpensive wines that are dangerously easy to drink.

How did it go?

Q The French seem to drink wine with every meal. Can that really be a wise habit to adopt?

A   *Yes, many do, but often the quantities consumed are negligible. A glass of wine is treated as part of the gastronomic fundamentals—alongside bread and water, oil and vinegar.*

Q I'm rather confused. In some respects wine seems to be beneficial. In others it seems incredibly damaging. What are we supposed to believe?

A   *There is no doubt that excessive alcohol consumption has a detrimental effect upon health. If it had been invented in the twentieth century it would almost certainly have been banned. But all studies into health constitute an inexact science. You have to make up your own mind about what you consider safe levels of consumption—and what risks you are prepared to take.*

Q Are some people more at risk than others?

A   *Yes. What complicates the matter is that alcohol consumption affects us all in different ways. Much depends on our size, gender, and metabolism.*

36

Eastern promise

In the eighteenth century Eastern Europe was home to some of the world's greatest wines. Yet 300 years later, the region labors under a reputation for producing rather indifferent wine. Will its star ever rise again?

There was a brief moment back in the '80s when it seemed that the time had come for the wines of Eastern Europe.

For years, producers in Hungary, Bulgaria, and Slovenia produced big, bold wines for the Soviet market that were just about palatable if drunk on a freezing cold night with a plate of goulash. However, the emergence of a new generation of fruitier, more commercial styles (that also had the advantage of being ludicrously cheap) made these producers feel they were on the brink of a renaissance. Soon a number of Eastern European wines—notably Bulgarian Cabernet Sauvignon—became a common sight on the tables of British wine drinkers. Foreign investors started to get involved—funding new wineries and planting familiar grape varieties such as Chardonnay, Sauvignon Blanc, Riesling, and Gewürztraminer. The future for the region's wine industry looked bright.

But in the mid-'90s this fledgling revival was stopped in its tracks. The hope was that Eastern Europe was going to offer drinkers wines that were more attractive

Here's an idea for you... **Such is the poor reputation of Eastern European wine that many people reject it out of hand. If you find an example that stands out well in a taste test try serving it to people blind. Rather than serving it from a bottle just produce a glass and judge your companions' reactions. Most drinkers are far more open-minded about wine if they can't see the label.**

than those from Germany and the South of France (which, at the time, were excelling at producing dull and undrinkable wines) and cheaper than those emerging from Australia, New Zealand, and California. But Eastern Europe's role as a source of cheap, palatable wines was thwarted by two factors—the lifting of sanctions upon the export of South African wines and the considerable investment in the Chilean industry—that resulted in lots of competition from a new generation of cheap, cheery wines from the southern hemisphere.

THE "BMS" THEORY AND EASTERN EUROPE

There is a theory—let's call it the "Bring Me Sunshine" theory—that drinkers are better disposed toward wines made in sunny countries where they might like to go on vacation than they are toward countries that they regard as chilly and, um, a little austere. If this is true, then it might explain the resistance to wines from Eastern Europe.

THE REVISIONIST THEORY ON EASTERN EUROPE

There are even those who seek to deny Eastern Europe's brief moment of fame. Their rewrite of oenological history goes something like this: The huge success of Eastern European wines—particularly those from Bulgaria—owed not to the prowess of winemakers in this region but to that of winemakers in the sunnier climes of South Africa. Bulgarian Cabernet Sauvignon, they believe, was not from Bulgaria at all. Rather, during the period that economic sanctions were imposed by many countries on South

Africa, wine from the Cape was shipped to Eastern Europe, where it was bottled as "Bulgarian." If that was the case, then it wouldn't have been the first time that such scams have been carried out: For years French producers regularly beefed up their own wines with wines from North Africa, especially Morocco.

One of the attractions of good Tokay is its combination of sweetness and acidity in equal measure. There is more on wines with these qualities in IDEA 4, *Sweet dreams*.

Try another idea...

TASTE TEST—THE REDS

Whatever prejudices you may have about Eastern Europe and its wines, the only way that you can judge them objectively is with blind tasting. Your prejudices might be confirmed, but—who knows?—they might instead be confounded.

■ Bulgarian Cabernet Sauvignon + inexpensive Chilean Cabernet Sauvignon + inexpensive southern French red

TASTE TEST—THE WHITES

■ Hungarian Sauvignon Blanc + Chilean Sauvignon Blanc + Hungarian Riesling + inexpensive German Riesling + Italian Pinot Grigio + inexpensive Australian Chardonnay

TOKAJI

"Nothing is as good as it seems beforehand."
GEORGE ELIOT, *Silas Marner*

Defining idea...

If you need evidence that Eastern Europe has the potential to make fabulous fine wines, you only have to look back 350 years to the Tokaj-

Hegyalja region in the northeast of Hungary. According to Hungarian mythology, an abbot, Mate Szepsi, ordered that the grape harvest be delayed because he feared an attack by the Turks. By the time that the grapes were harvested some of them had started to rot. These were picked separately and made into wine. Soon Tokaji (or "Tokay" as it is known in English-speaking countries) was one of Europe's most sought-after wines, famed for its delicate sweetness and enjoyed by the Russian and French courts as well as the Hapsburgs. It remains one of the world's most delicious wines.

How did it go? **Q**   **The Eastern European wines that I tasted came out of the taste test very well. Why is it that they were also substantially cheaper?**

A   *The answer lies in lower overheads. Land and labor in Eastern Europe tend to be cheaper than in most other wine-producing regions, so the wine is cheaper, too.*

Q   **Why have Eastern European wines improved so much in the last twenty years?**

A   *For the same reasons that they have improved in France and Germany. More investment and better technology mean that it is now possible to make good wine almost anywhere in the world that vines will grow.*

Q   **Why did Tokay fall into obscurity if it was once so sought after?**

A   *Partly because of lack of investment and also because sweet styles of wine aren't as popular as they once were.*

37

Touch me in the morning

Is Port little more than a guaranteed path to a hangover? Or is it one of the world's most artfully made wines? You decide.

One of the great enduring myths about Port is that it is guaranteed to cause a hangover. The reason for this is quite simple.

Imagine the typical intake of alcohol on an indulgent evening—say, a glass or two of Champagne, a glass of white with a starter, a couple of glasses of red with the main course. Almost without thinking about it you have drunk the equivalent of a bottle of wine—and quite a mixture at that. Embark now on a glass of Port and the mixture becomes even more toxic, almost guaranteeing a throbbing head in the morning. The next day your memory is of the last drink spotted at the scene of the crime—and so it is Port that gets the blame.

To understand any drink you need to start by studying it in isolation. Like Champagne, Port is one of those drinks that tends to be shrouded in the myths that surround it. But just as Champagne is simply a wine enlivened with bubbles, Port is simply a wine that has been given an alcoholic kick by the addition of grape spirit. And, like Sauternes and some of Germany's finest wines, it suffers from the problem

Here's an idea for you...

Port tends to have such an overbearing flavor that it needs to be paired with foods with similarly assertive flavors. Find the right combination and it could do much to enhance your enjoyment of this drink. Start with classic accompaniments such as almonds or blue cheese and then try rich desserts such as chocolate. Alternatively, something as simple as a slice of melon can work wonders.

associated with all sweet wines: prejudice. This is quite understandable—bad Port has little to recommend it—but the problem is not one of sweetness but of quality.

STYLES OF PORT

- *Vintage Port* is made from the best grapes from a particularly good harvest and becomes increasingly mellow with age.
- *Tawny Port* is aged in oak casks for ten, twenty, or thirty years before bottling.
- *Colheita* is tawny Port from a single vintage.
- *Late-bottled* vintage Port is aged for four to six years in cask.

VINTAGE PORT AND THE ART OF AGING GRACEFULLY

For devotees of vintage Port one of its greatest attractions is its capacity to develop with age. While the flavors of most whites start to subside after two or three years and those of reds last only a few more, the robust ingredients in Port give it a staying power that means it will continue to develop for decades. Considering both its quality and its age, vintage Port offers very good value for those who like long-lived wines—and even if the contents of a glass aren't outstanding, there is the novelty of knowing that you are drinking a wine that has become part of vinous history.

TASTE TEST

Explore the different styles in a tasting and you might start to see Port not as a sickly sweet drink that you consume when you are already inebriated but simply as yet another style of wine. Line up the following wines:

- Inexpensive Port + late-bottled vintage Port that is at least ten years old + tawny Port (served slightly chilled) + a sweetish style of New World Cabernet + a dry red (e.g., Burgundy)

COMPARE AND CONTRAST

The main aim is to assess the balance between sweetness and any other flavors you might find. Look, too, at the relationship between color and flavor.

THE WHITE STUFF

Though the people who make Port are enthusiastic drinkers of their own wine, the last thing that anyone would want to sip on a terrace at the end of a hot day in the Douro Valley is a tepid glass of vintage Port. The answer? White Port—a curious wine that is made from white grapes in almost exactly the same way as red Port is made. Mixed with ice and tonic it is a cool, refreshing drink with a wonderfully tangy, palate-enlivening flavor.

The subject of sweetness in wine is a vexed one. There's more discussion of this topic in IDEA 4, *Sweet dreams.*

Try another idea...

"*I have often thought that the aim of port is to give you a good and durable hangover, so during the next day you should be reminded of the splendid occasion that you had the night before.*"
GEORGE MIKES

Defining idea...

163

How did
it go?

Q   Why is it that the late-bottled vintage Port has more flavor than the vintage and tawny Port?

A   *Probably because it is younger. It's a style that is not just cheaper than vintage and tawny Port but can also have a much more robust flavor. The style that you choose is really up to your own personal taste. The mellower flavors of vintage and tawny tend to appeal to the British palate whereas the more forthright style of younger Port is more popular in America.*

Q   Why is tawny Port much paler in color?

A   *Because it is aged in casks, where it becomes paler and more mellow.*

Q   White Port sounds a little strange. Is it?

A   *White Port is an oddity, but as a free-thinking drinker you should be influenced not by the image of a wine but by its flavor. Try some.*

38

The brave New World

Wine buffs use the term "New World" as though Christopher Columbus had only just discovered that there was human life beyond the Atlantic. But outdated or not, it is a convenient description to refer to a revolutionary new approach to wine.

Anyone new to the business of wine appreciation might be confused by the way that a variety of disparate wine regions in the Americas and the southern hemisphere are bunched together under this all-encompassing term "New World."

These include Australia, New Zealand, South Africa, Chile, and California. From the lips of a British wine merchant of the old school the term can sound deeply patronizing. It seems to imply that not only are these countries still in their infancy but so, too, are their winemaking skills. In fact, wine has been made in many New World regions for hundreds of years. An early Dutch governor of South Africa, Simon van der Stel, established a vineyard in that country way back in 1685. The resulting wine was not merely a commodity to peddle to sailors on the busy trade route around the Cape; it became one of the world's most sought after, whose

Whenever you try a wine blind, try to identify whether it is from the Old World or the New World. The number of times that you get it wrong might make you decide that these terms no longer have much relevance.

many fans included Napoleon. Other New World wine regions have similarly impressive histories. Wine has been made in Australia since the early nineteenth century and in California winemaking flourished to supply the huge number of prospectors drawn to the region by the great Gold Rush of the 1850s. Yet the way some wine buffs talk you might be excused for thinking that wine has only been made in these regions for a decade or two.

The term "New World" is really shorthand and refers more to the different climates and philosophies that distinguish New World wines from those made in the Old World.

A SHORT HISTORY OF NEW WORLD WINEMAKING

Although wine has been made in some New World areas for two or three centuries, few have a tradition of making good quality wine that dates back much further than fifty years. Previously, producers in regions such as Australia, California, Chile, and South Africa made sweet, fortified wines for customers who ran on heavy fuel. However, after World War II, growing affluence and more foreign travel encouraged a new generation of consumers with a more sophisticated palate that favored dry wines over sweet. In addition, the realization that it is possible to make good quality table wines outside Europe encouraged pioneering winemakers to start catering for new consumers. Within a decade or so the global wine market was transformed beyond all recognition.

TASTE TEST

Even if you've already performed the following comparisons in another context, for the purposes of understanding the differences between New World and Old World wines carefully compare the following:

- Australian Cabernet + aged, Cabernet-based red Bordeaux
- Chablis + Australian Chardonnay

SPOT THE DIFFERENCE

- New World wines have the name of the grape on the bottle. Old World wines don't.
- New World wines tend to be made from just one grape variety. Old World wines are often made from a blend.
- New World wines offer plenty of information on the label. Old World wines offer very little.

In the past, one of the main differences between winemaking in the Old World and in the New World was the belief in terroir–the idea that wine should reflect the soil and climate of the landscape in which it is produced. There's more of this in IDEA 17, *The reign of terroir.*

Try another idea...

"I called the New World into existence to redress the balance of the old."
GEORGE CANNING, former British prime minister

Defining idea...

A QUESTION OF TASTE

But the differences aren't just about labeling. They are also about flavors that result from different climates and approaches to winemaking. From the results of the taste test try to define exactly what sets the New World and the Old World apart.

NEW-STYLE OLD WORLD WINES

Because of the success of New World wines many European wine producers have set out to mimic their style. The result is that you'll find wines from regions such as the South of France, Italy, and Eastern Europe that are almost identical in style and have similar labels to wines from Australia, Chile, and New Zealand. Nothing's simple, is it?

THE GRAPE DEBATE

Hardened fans of Old World wines criticize New World wines for being too simple, lacking in character, and all tasting the same—"homogeneous" is a word you'll often hear them use when talking about wine from Australia and Chile. Devotees of New World wines believe that "character" is simply an excuse for sloppy winemaking and that the best wines are those that maximize the flavor and aroma of the grapes. Of course, such arguments tend to massively oversimplify the facts and rely on sweeping generalizations. The free-thinking drinker knows that when it comes to wine there are plenty of exceptions to every rule.

Q **Is the character of typical Old World wines really the result of sloppy winemaking?**

How did it go?

A *In the past this might have been the case. But these days the accusation is purely mischievous. The difference between Old World and New World wines has more to do with style preferences.*

Q **Is there anything wrong with Old World wines that mimic the style of New World wines?**

A *Nothing at all. However, they are of less interest to wine enthusiasts because they don't reflect the region where they were made; they could have been made anywhere.*

39

All fine and dandy

What makes a wine worthy of the description "fine"? A fancy label (and price to match) or a delicious flavor and aroma? As a free-thinking drinker you'll soon discover the answer to this question—and also that fine wines needn't break the bank.

The word "fine" has the capacity to transform the image of a wine from being a humble agricultural product to the result of artistic endeavor.

Yet, "fine" is a deeply subjective term that could be used to describe the contents of any bottle, whether it be the product of a winery with all the charm of an oil refinery or the product of a small vineyard where wine is painstakingly crafted to make it as close to perfection as humanly possible. So what does "fine" mean? Is it simply used to justify high prices or is it a genuinely useful term that offers some guarantee of quality? In order to explore this subject it is essential that the free-thinking drinker distinguishes two very different sorts of wine.

Here's an idea for you... **Try comparing an expensive, prestigious fine wine with a favorite, more offbeat wine from the South of France or Spain. Consider the difference in price and then decide whether or not it's really worth the extra expense.**

EVERYDAY WINE

It doesn't sound great, does it? Yet the term "everyday wine" is useful shorthand for wine that is of basic quality—simple, attractive, and a good all-around companion to food. The quality of everyday wine has improved dramatically in the last twenty years. Better winemaking methods have made the quality of basic wine better than ever before, and because of the spread of winemaking all over the world it is now more plentiful—and therefore cheaper—than ever before.

There are two different types of everyday wine. One is "global everyday wine," which is usually made from well-known grape varieties such as Chardonnay and Cabernet and tastes the same wherever it is made. The other is "country-specific everyday wine"—most of it made in Europe—that reflects the winemaking culture of the region in which it was produced. Which style you choose is simply a question of your own personal taste—or perhaps the food you are eating (e.g., a basic typical Italian red might taste better with spaghetti Bolognese than would a fruity Chilean Merlot).

FINE WINE

This sort of wine aims to reflect one or more of the following:
- The climate and soil of the landscape where it was made
- The grape—or grapes—from which it was made
- The year in which it was made

In order to achieve any one of these qualities it is essential that the wine is made with care and from the highest-quality grapes. But remember that a fine wine won't necessarily offer more sensual enjoyment than an everyday wine. Tasting it might be more of an intellectual challenge, but it won't necessarily be as enjoyable as a simple bottle with steak and fries.

TASTE TEST

The following test includes comparisons that you may have performed in other taste tests, but for the purposes of this subject it is good to explore them again:

- Expensive red Bordeaux from a vintage in the early '90s + expensive Australian Shiraz + inexpensive Chilean Merlot + inexpensive but attractive Valpolicella

COMPARE AND CONTRAST

This lineup includes examples of fine wines, as well as global wines and country-specific everyday wines. Try marking the wines when you are tasting them blind so that you can compare them with their prices.

You might discover wines that are technically "fine" but that you don't find especially attractive—particularly among those from Australia. One of the disadvantages of the very competitive nature of the Australian winemaking industry is that many wines are made to display pronounced flavors and aromas that will stand out in competitions, but these aren't necessarily the same wines that you might want to spend an evening with.

One of the advantages of fine wines is that their flavors and aromas evolve with a few years in the bottle—a quality that fascinates hardened wine buffs. There's more on this in IDEA 14, *Growing old gracefully*.

Try another idea...

"Wine is art. It's culture, it's the essence of civilization."
ROBERT MONDAVI, Californian winemaker

Defining idea...

173

THE PRICE OF FINE WINE

Don't allow yourself to be conned into thinking that all fine wines have fancy names and fancy prices. Wine can be expensive for a variety of reasons. It might simply be a rarity, or have been given a glowing but misjudged endorsement by an influential wine critic—in fact, all sorts of reasons that have little to do with the flavor of the wine in the bottle. Equally, wine can be inexpensive but delicious, perhaps because it is heavily discounted or because it comes from a region where there is over-supply. Though you will pay a premium for wines from a prestigious producer, it is quite possible to find beautifully crafted wines in more offbeat regions such as the South of France and Spain.

How did it go?

Q **Why do fine red wines tend to age after a couple of years in the bottle whereas everyday wines will deteriorate?**

A *Essentially because of the quality of the grapes but also because of the more painstaking process used to make them.*

Q **Do fine white wines improve with age?**

A *Only a few, such as Sauternes. Some people like old white Burgundy and old Champagne, but they tend to be an eccentric bunch.*

Q **If some fine wines aren't very attractive to drink, why do they sell for high prices?**

A *Because they are expensive to make. Besides, you'd be amazed how much money people will pay for bad wine.*

40

Simply reds

Cabernet Sauvignon, Merlot, Shiraz, and Pinot Noir might have achieved world domination, but once you've mastered them, get your head around the flavors that grapes such as Malbec, Cabernet Franc, Pinotage, Zinfandel, and Carmenere have to offer.

It's easy to become lazy in one's approach to wine. Find a few grapes and styles that you like from a few reputable producers and it's easy never to stray much beyond the familiar territory of the familiar names.

But variety is essential if you want to achieve vinous nirvana. Discovering new flavors and aromas is an essential part of wine appreciation. The reason that a relatively small number of grapes have achieved such a monopoly over our palates is that they are tried and tested. The longer that winemakers work with them, the deeper their knowledge becomes and the greater the opportunities they have to exploit these grapes to their full potential. What is more exciting is when little-known grapes—or ones that have played unsung roles in other wines—come to the fore and are used to create previously unknown flavors and aromas.

Here's an idea for you... One of the most exciting aspects of finding a new flavor or aroma in a wine that you didn't know existed is that it offers new possibilities when it comes to matching food and wine. As well as comparing these offbeat wines, try matching them to a variety of different foods. You'll be amazed at the successful pairings you'll discover.

OFFBEAT RED GRAPES

- *Cabernet Franc.* Often seen as Cabernet Sauvignon's poor relation, this grape makes wonderful wine in the Loire and, increasingly, in Australia, South America, and California.

- *Carmenere.* This wonderful grape is enjoying a revival—particularly in Chile, where it produces big, structured wines not dissimilar in style to Cabernet. It is thought to have originated in Bordeaux.

- *Malbec.* Another French grape variety that is enjoying a renaissance in South America. In southwest France it is the key ingredient in wines such as Cahors, but in Chile and Argentina it creates wonderfully lush wines that make good alternatives to red Bordeaux.

- *Pinotage.* A real Frankenstein grape created in South Africa in the '20s by crossing Pinot Noir with Cinsault. It is making wonderful robust reds of increasing sophistication.

- *Zinfandel.* Little is known about the origins of this robust grape variety that California has made famous.

TASTE TEST

- Argentinian Cabernet Franc + Chilean Malbec + South African Pinotage + Californian Zinfandel + Chilean Carmenere

To put these wines in context, compare them with a Cabernet Sauvignon that you know very well.

COMPARE AND CONTRAST

As you will have discovered, there's a great deal more to red wine than you thought. One of the greatest benefits of the New World wine revolution is that it has encouraged wine lovers to see a number of grapes in a completely new light. The reason the wines are so different is not just the different climate but also the pioneering spirit of winemakers in places like Australia, Chile, and California. In many cases New World winemakers are teaching those in the Old World about the unexploited potential of grapes that they had previously overlooked.

If you enjoy tasting offbeat red wines, try exploring offbeat whites that offer a similarly stimulating experience, as in IDEA 9, *Whites with attitude*.

Try another idea...

"Be not forgetful to entertain strangers: for thereby some have entertained angels unaware."
HEBREWS 13:2

Defining idea...

How did it go?

Q   Why do some of the offbeat reds seem a little assertive for my tastes?

A   *Probably because you aren't used to them. Remember how weird and wonderful wine tasted when you took your first ever sip? The more you taste, the more tame the wines will begin to appear. Persevere.*

Q   Why is it that all the offbeat grapes suggested in the taste test come from New World countries?

A   *Because in Europe offbeat grapes tend to be blended with other grapes. In wines from countries such as Australia you get them unadulterated.*

Q   Why don't European winemakers make more wines that contain just one grape variety?

A   *Because they believe that the area where a wine is made is more important than the grapes themselves. They like to make wines that are typical of a region rather than of a grape.*

41

Hot off the starting line

Australia, New Zealand, and California might have had a head start in the race to create fabulous, world-class wines, but South Africa and Chile aren't far behind.

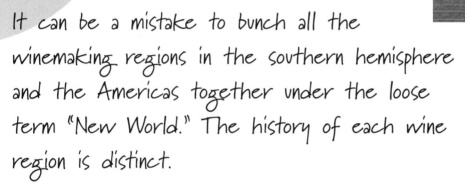

It can be a mistake to bunch all the winemaking regions in the southern hemisphere and the Americas together under the loose term "New World." The history of each wine region is distinct.

Each has developed at a different speed and recent successes have resulted from very different factors. The recent history of South Africa's wine industry, for example, is tied up with its political history. Although wine has been made in the Cape for over 300 years, for much of the late twentieth century the development of winemaking was stunted by political and economic isolation. For a developing wine industry to flourish it's essential that it be open to outside influences—both from other developing regions and from the "mother ship" regions in Europe, where there's centuries of accumulated oenological expertise. Winemakers in South Africa had no such luxury. Both quality and innovation were also hindered by strict regulations and a dominant cooperative system. The result is that, despite its

Here's an idea for you... **Both Carmenere and Pinotage make excellent partners for food, particularly grilled red meat. Try experimenting in matching their pronounced flavors with dishes that you might otherwise serve with Cabernet or Pinot Noir.**

centuries-old history, winemaking in South Africa didn't fulfill its potential until the '90s, when the first free elections precipitated closer ties with the rest of the world and brought economic sanctions to an end.

Similarly, a new democratic political climate in Chile precipitated the leaping advances in the country's wine industry in the '80s. Although the Chilean and South African winemakers had a much slower start than those in Australia, New Zealand, and California, they have caught up with astonishing alacrity. In both Chile and South Africa foreign investment (by some of the most prestigious names in the French wine industry) and exposure to new ideas and vine varieties have created exponential improvements. In the mid-'90s both countries were associated with basic supermarket wines of inferior quality than those produced in Australia and New Zealand and it seemed like they had missed the boat. Today, though Chile and South Africa do produce some excellent, inexpensive wines, the following taste tests will reveal that this is not the end of the story.

TASTE TEST—THE REDS

- Mid-price Chilean Carmenere + mid-price South African Cabernet or Cabernet-based blend + mid-price Pinotage + similarly priced Cabernet-based Bordeaux + similarly priced Californian Cabernet

TASTE TEST—THE WHITES

- Good quality examples of the following: Chilean Chardonnay + South African Chardonnay + Chilean Sauvignon Blanc + New Zealand Sauvignon Blanc + Australian Chardonnay

COMPARE AND CONTRAST

In these tests it is important to compare the prices of the wines to see which you feel offer the best value for money—and also to see whether there are any significant differences in style between the different wines.

If you enjoy alternatives to predictable grapes such as Cabernet and Merlot, there's more on offbeat varieties in IDEA 40, *Simply reds.*

Try another idea...

SPOT THE DIFFERENCE?

Some of the wines that you've tasted may have seemed very similar in style. Perhaps you felt that they simply tasted like very typical New World Chardonnay, Sauvignon, or Cabernet. There is an argument that with the growing globalization of the wine industry the origin of a wine is becoming less important. At one level this seems a valid argument; basic Chilean Chardonnay won't taste much different from Chardonnay made in South Africa, Australia, or northern Italy (in fact, the only difference might be in price). At a more elevated level, the discovery of new regions that are well suited to certain grape varieties has created wines with unique qualities, such as Chardonnays from the South African region of Robertson and wonderfully glossy Cabernets from Rapel in Chile.

UNIQUE SELLING POINT GRAPES

It is with offbeat grapes that regions such as South Africa and Chile are creating their own identity. Both Chile and South Africa have wines that they've succeeded in making their own. In Chile, there's Carmenere—a previously obscure grape variety that is thought to have

"While overseas contact has awakened South African winemakers to new possibilities, they are not afraid to express the uniqueness of what is their own."
SU BIRCH, CEO of Wines of South Africa

Defining idea...

181

originated from Bordeaux—and Pinotage, a hybrid grape created by crossing Pinot Noir with Cinsault.

PUTTING SOUTH AFRICAN AND CHILEAN WINES IN CONTEXT

Like any other type of wine, it pays to taste South African wines in the context of the gastronomic tradition of the countries where they are made. The reds, particularly, are well-suited to boldly flavored grilled meat.

How did it go?

Q If wine has been made in South Africa for 300 years why has it taken so long to create high-quality table wines?

A   *Winemakers are led by demand. For much of the twentieth century the domestic markets in South Africa, and Australia, too, were quite happy with sweetish or very robust wines.*

Q Why is it that basic Chilean and South African wines are cheaper than those from Australia and New Zealand?

A   *Largely because overheads in the first two countries are lower. But these two countries don't have a monopoly on good-value wines. Spain, France, the US, and Italy also produce excellent inexpensive wines.*

Q Why are there so many good-value wines from California, where overheads are high?

A   *There are other factors that can influence the price of wine, such as over-supply and currency fluctuations.*

42

The lure of the Loire

Of all the French wine regions that have received a serious challenge from New World winemakers it is the Loire Valley that has been the most guilty of complacency.

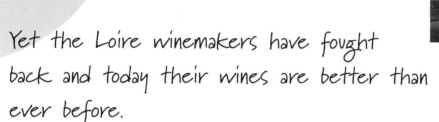

Yet the Loire winemakers have fought back and today their wines are better than ever before.

Sometimes it takes a shock to shake a wine region out of apathy. In the '80s the Loire Valley—like Bordeaux and Burgundy—was resting on its laurels. Its reputation for quality had been firmly established for many years and never questioned by an adoring public dazzled by the fancy labels and swanky names. But with the coming of the New World winemaking revolution, it was the Loire that was most exposed to competition—largely from energetic young winemakers in New Zealand.

Winemakers in the Loire believed that they had an effective monopoly over a grape that they believed was their own—Sauvignon Blanc. Yet New Zealand winemakers were discovering that the grape thrived in their own climate. This fact—combined with the New Zealand industry's exceptional technological expertise—created Sauvignons that put those from the grape's spiritual home in the shade. When winemakers in the Loire woke up to the fact that their wines were being eclipsed

Here's an idea for you... **The Loire is a complex wine region for which you will require a detailed map to help you find the places behind the names. Whenever tasting a wine from the Loire ensure that you have identified its precise location on a map.**

by New World upstarts, they quickly began to clean up their act. In the finest cases the new generation of Loire Sauvignons—notably Pouilly Fume and Sancerre—offer the best of both worlds. They combine the freshness of New Zealand Sauvignon with the minerally grace and charm associated with many of the best French wines.

TASTE TEST 1

- Inexpensive Touraine Sauvignon + inexpensive Chilean Sauvignon + inexpensive New Zealand Sauvignon + good-quality Sancerre or Pouilly Fume + good-quality New Zealand Sauvignon Blanc

COMPARE AND CONTRAST

In this test you should see Sauvignon in its multitude of different guises, which can range from thin and watery to rich, opulent, and three-dimensional. Which do you like most and which do you think offer the best value for the money?

BEYOND SAUVIGNON

Although the Loire is most famous for its Sauvignons the region also offers a number of underrated red and white wines. If you get confused by the complicated lists of names, try exploring the region's wines through the perspective of the principal grape varieties:

- Melon de Bourgogne (Muscadet)
- Chenin Blanc (Vouvray)
- Cabernet Franc (Chinon and Bourgueil)

Of course, plenty of other wines are made in this diverse region, but, for the purposes of weeding out, these are the wines with which you should try to familiarize yourself first.

New Zealand's challenge to the Loire Valley's monopoly over the Sauvignon Blanc grape is explored in greater detail in IDEA 27, *Fantasy island*.

Try another idea...

For fresh, neutral whites, Muscadet is a good wine to explore. In the past it had a reputation for being insipid, poor quality swill but increasingly it is delivering both character and value for the money. For many accustomed to the assertive flavors of New World whites, Muscadet might seem a little restrained, but serve it with seafood or subtle fish dishes and you may think differently. The other major white grape variety, Chenin Blanc, might have a poor reputation outside the Loire but it is really the grape at which producers in areas such as Vouvray excel—particularly when they use it to make wines with a delicate, honeyed sweetness. The most successful red grape variety, Cabernet Franc, is becoming increasingly popular in the New World, but don't overlook those from the Loire; they are an exceptionally good value for the money and a superb accompaniment to food.

"Failure is not the only punishment for laziness; There is also the success of others."
JULES RENARD, French writer

Defining idea...

TASTE TEST 2

To put the wines into context try the following lineups:

- Good-quality Muscadet + basic Chilean Sauvignon Blanc + basic northern Italian white
- Good-quality medium sweet Vouvray + Alsace Gewurztraminer + inexpensive Australian Chardonnay
- Chinon or Bourgueil Cabernet Franc + Australian Shiraz

THE LOIRE'S COOL REDS

The leafy, assertive character of Loire reds such as those from Chinon and Bourgueil lend themselves to being served at a similar temperature to white wines—they make a refreshing accompaniment to grilled meat on a hot summer's day.

Q **I was surprised not just by the excellent quality of the Sauvignons from some of the better-known areas of the Loire but also by those from Touraine, which seem a very good value for the money compared with many of those from the New World. Why is it that wines from this region are so often overlooked?**

How did it go?

A *The same is true of so many French wines. Because New World producers have been so successful at marketing their wines, wines such as Touraine Sauvignon have been left by the wayside. You are discovering the infinite joys of being a free-thinking drinker.*

A **Is the same true of the reds from Chinon and Bourgeuil?**

A *Yes—although their particular attraction is that they also offer unique qualities, such as a wonderful leafy richness.*

Q **Muscadet seems a little too neutral for my taste. Why is it enjoying a revival?**

A *Partly because the quality is improving, but also because many wine lovers are beginning to appreciate those wines that are the antithesis of the in-your-face style of many New World whites. There are times when neutral whites such as Muscadet are just what is called for—especially when you're eating food with subtle flavors.*

43

A river runs through it

The vineyards that stretch down to the Rhône produce some of the world's most delicious reds—and also one of the most legendary whites. But the Rhône's greatest success has been to remain true to its winemaking tradition.

In recent years the classic winemaking regions of France, such as Bordeaux, Burgundy, and the Loire, have responded to New World competition in different ways.

Some producers in Bordeaux have tried to compete by creating brands that they hope will succeed in matching those from Australia—although in many cases these have been a triumph of style over substance. In Burgundy, the response of most winemakers has been to keep their heads firmly in the sand and continue producing a combination of thin, unattractive wines and some fabulous vintages that are beyond the reach of all but the extremely wealthy. In the Loire, producers have swiftly cleaned up their act and now produce better wines than ever before.

But producers in the Rhône Valley have taken an altogether more courageous approach. Rather than burying their heads or following fashion, they have simply

Here's an idea for you...

Hearty Rhône reds aren't made to be drunk on their own— compare your reactions to a Rhône red, first by tasting it alone and then in the company of food. You'll be amazed at the difference . . .

had faith in their ability to create some of the world's greatest wines, ranging from simple, cockle-warming everyday wines to sublime, complex Hermitage and Chateauneuf du Pape. The result is that they have succeeded in leading rather than following. While winemakers in other French wine regions have tried to mimic the hugely successful style of Australian Shiraz (a wine made from the Rhône's classic red grape, Syrah), the Rhône's winemakers have made a huge effort to improve what they were already doing—with stunning results.

A WHISTLESTOP TOUR DOWN THE RHÔNE

The Rhône River stretches all the way from Switzerland to France's deep hot south. For simplicity, it is useful to split the region in two: the northern Rhône and southern Rhône.

The northern Rhône is where the Syrah grape holds sway, producing fabulous individual wines such as Cote Rotie, Hermitage, St. Joseph, Crozes Hermitage, and Cornas. It's also here that the white Viognier grape has its spiritual home in the tiny region of Condrieu, where it makes magnificent sensual wines with an almost mythical reputation.

As the river heads to the warmer south, the wines get beefier, ranging from simple Cotes du Rhône to complex Chateauneuf du Pape. These derive much of their charm from the fact that they are made from a range of grapes, including Mourvedre, Cinsault, and Carignan.

THE PERFECT WINTER WINE

Rhône reds could have been made for chilly winter evenings. The combination of spicy, warming flavors to be found in a good Chateauneuf du Pape might seem incongruous on a sweltering evening in July—but in the depths of February, they offer more comfort and succour than any red Bordeaux or Australian Cabernet. It is for this reason that a ballsy Rhône red is considered the classic partner to hearty stews.

If Rhône Syrah doesn't appeal, then try its New World incarnation, known as "Shiraz" which has been exceptionally successful in Australia. For more on the subject turn to IDEA 31, *Que Syrah, Syrah.* *Try another idea...*

TASTE TEST

The following tasting will demonstrate the variety of styles offered by the region.

■ Good-quality Hermitage + good-quality Chateauneuf du Pape + good-quality Cotes du Rhône + basic Cotes du Rhône + good-quality Australian Shiraz + inexpensive Australian Cabernet Sauvignon

COMPARE AND CONTRAST

Although the Syrah grape dominates the Rhône, the region's wines are not about grapes: They are about rich flavors, sun, and soil.
Nevertheless, comparing them closely with single-variety wines such as Australian Cabernet Sauvignon and Shiraz should make you see them in a very different light.

"What the superior man seeks is in himself: What the small man seeks is in others."
CONFUCIUS, *Analects*

Defining idea...

THE RHÔNE WANNABES

The style of Rhône wines has been widely copied by droves of New World producers. In California, Rhône-style blends offer an alternative to the monotony of single-variety reds such as Cabernet and Merlot, and in South Africa one producer has been so eager to pay homage to the region that he has produced a wine called Goats du Roam.

VIOGNIER

The tiny Rhône Valley region of Condrieu is where the fabulously scented quality and luscious texture of the Viognier grape are perfectly expressed. However, the quality of Viognier—both from Condrieu and elsewhere—can be enormously variable and a truly delicious example tends to be the exception rather than the rule. Nevertheless, find a good example and you could be at the start of a lifelong love affair.

Q I love the warming flavors of good Cotes du Rhône. What is the secret behind its charm?

A *A combination of warm climate and blending. As in many French wines, the combination of grapes to be found in Cotes du Rhône is far, far more than the sum of its parts.*

Q I find Australian Shiraz more approachable than most of the northern Rhône reds that I've tasted. Why is this?

A *Probably because you are used to the sunnier, fruitier style of Australian reds. At first, Rhône reds can be a little more demanding.*

Q Why is Condrieu so expensive?

A *Because only a small amount of it is made. The price of a wine is often related to supply and demand—though the fact that it's expensive doesn't mean it is necessarily any good.*

How did it go?

44

The great Burgundy test

In Burgundy, the Pinot Noir and Chardonnay grapes are ingredients of some of the world's most revered wines. But have winemakers elsewhere had more success in using them to create everyday wines?

Old World wine buffs are roughly split into two groups: those who love red Bordeaux and those who love red Burgundy.

Bordeaux, it is said, attracts the intellectuals, the lovers of order, logic, and hierarchy. Red Burgundy, on the other hand, is supposed to attract the sensualists. When you first stumble upon a good one (no doubt having paid a huge amount of money for the pleasure of doing so) you will come to realize that tasting and smelling great red Burgundy is a life-changing experience.

THE THRILL OF THE CHASE

But taste a *bad* Burgundian Pinot Noir and you might be wondering what particular aspect of it is supposed to be sensual. There is no doubt that much of the grape's appeal lies in its inconsistency. For many wine lovers, finding good Burgundian Pinot Noir is like finding truffles—it combines gastronomy with the thrill of the chase. For winemakers, it offers a similar challenge. This notoriously fickle grape

Here's an idea for you...

However disappointing basic red Burgundy might appear on first taste, it is a good example of a French wine that tastes far better with food than on its own. Try drinking it with a typical dish of the region such as boeuf bourguignon.

variety is the petulant prima donna of the grape world and can create good and bad wines in equal measure.

In Burgundy, the hallowed ground that is regarded as the spiritual home of Pinot Noir is the Côte d'Or. To hardened old-school wine buffs the vineyards of this tiny area are the only places where it is possible to make truly great Pinot Noir. Yet despite the grape's reputation, a number of winemakers in other wine regions with a similarly cool, temperate climate, such as in New Zealand, Australia, Oregon, California, and Germany, have had great success in creating fabulous perfumed wines with this grape. There are some parallels with the success that New World winemakers have achieved with Shiraz: though they haven't succeeded in creating exact replicas of Rhône reds, they have used the grape to create a style of wine that is all their own. So, though the wines made from Pinot Noir in other regions might not have the extraordinary haunting character of great red Burgundy, many have a wonderful, highly distinctive freshness.

TASTE TEST 1

- Good-quality red Burgundy + basic red Burgundy + good-quality New Zealand Pinot Noir + good-quality Pinot Noir from either California or Oregon

COMPARE AND CONTRAST

There is a good chance that the wines in this tasting will lead you to an emphatic conclusion: that in the right hands and the right conditions the Pinot Noir grape can be used to make great wines anywhere in the world.

196

The Côte de Beaune is to Chardonnay what the Côte d'Or is to Pinot Noir. But to buy the wines at their best you need to dig deep into your pocket. However, Chardonnay is a more versatile grape than Pinot Noir and creates a much wider range of styles, from simple and refreshing to impressively complex.

There is more on New Zealand Pinot Noir in IDEA 27, *Fantasy island*, and on Chardonnay in IDEA 8, *Understanding Chardonnay.*

Try another idea...

TASTE TEST 2

- Good-quality white Burgundy + good-quality Californian Chardonnay + mid-range South African Chardonnay

COMPARE AND CONTRAST

How does breathtakingly expensive white Burgundy stand up to the competition? Even if it is better, is it worth the extra investment?

THE FIRST TASTE IS THE SWEETEST

You might spend years trying to find the perfect expression of Burgundian Pinot Noir and Chardonnay. On your journey, there's every chance that you'll experience wines that have all the charm of rotten cabbage and others that taste like battery acid. But once you've tasted a great example, you will be prepared to embark on the same exhaustive process in order to find another. The question you'll have to ask yourself is whether it is worth the investment—for every twenty wines you taste, there is a

"The thin skinned, early ripening Pinot Noir is undoubtedly more difficult to grow than other varieties like Cabernet or Chardonnay but that doesn't mean that it is impossible to grow elsewhere—you just have to work at it with more sensitivity and seek out the right growing conditions."
OZ CLARKE

Defining idea...

197

chance that you might only taste one good example. One of the reasons that New World wines have been so successful in recent years is because they tend to be more consistent—only time will teach you which is the most sensible path to follow.

POOR MAN'S CHABLIS

Though inexpensive white Burgundy can be very disappointing, many would opt for the good-value whites to be found farther south in the Maconnais. These offer the combination of the prestige of white Burgundy with crisp, racy flavors.

How did it go?

Q Why is it that the New Zealand Pinot Noir has a fuller, richer flavor than the example from Burgundy?

A *Partly because of climate and partly because of winemaking. The other advantages of New World Pinot Noirs are that they tend to be cheaper and more consistent.*

Q Why is Burgundian Chardonnay often so disappointing?

A *It really has to do with climate—and the fact that we are now so used to much sunnier styles of Chardonnay.*

Q The Macon seemed better than the basic white Burgundy I tried but it was still very disappointing. What would you say to that?

A *You should probably avoid white Burgundy altogether. A huge number of people do.*

45

The great white hope

The Semillon grape is one of the wine world's best kept secrets and makes some of the world's most alluring wines. Allow its offbeat flavors and aromas to enhance your gastronomic life.

There are many covert signs that identify a wine buff. One is the fact that they always hold a glass of wine by its stem.

Another is that when they try wine in a restaurant they do so simply by smelling it rather than tasting it. Yet another is a passion for Semillon, a wine that to the uninitiated can taste strangely flabby compared with Chardonnay, Sauvignon, or Riesling. But few grapes reward perseverance like Semillon. With experience, what once might have seemed flabby begins to seem rich and opulent and, in some cases, utterly beguiling, especially with age.

A SHORT HISTORY OF SEMILLON

The grape is thought to have originated in the Sauternes region of Bordeaux, where in the eighteenth century it was used to make sweet wines that are now world famous. Its cultivation then spread all over Bordeaux and became the region's classic white grape, such as Sauvignon Blanc in the Loire and Chardonnay in

Here's an idea for you... **Semillon has the potential to completely transform your experience of certain types of food. Try experimenting with the different styles in conjunction with a variety of different flavors. Try drinking a dry white Semillon-based Bordeaux with fish and seafood, or sweet Semillon with rich, creamy sauces and blue cheese. Semillon can also make a great partner to spicy food.**

Burgundy. In the nineteenth century it was widely planted all over South America and South Africa, where it made flavorless wines of spectacular dullness that were either blended or distilled. In the 1970s it was taken up in the New World, particularly in Australia, where its star has risen dramatically.

WHAT MAKES SEMILLON DIFFERENT?

Most modern drinkers are now programmed to expect two flavors from a white wine; on the one hand there is the slightly sweet tropical character of New World Chardonnay and on the other, the crisp, acidic character of Sauvignon Blanc and Burgundian Chardonnay. The absence of either of these qualities in a white wine can come as quite a shock, notably in the case of wines such as white Rioja, as well as various Italian whites such as Soave that seem to buck the trend. Instead, many Semillons might seem almost flavorless and inert at first. However, closer attention will reveal a variety of other qualities ranging from a soft nuttiness to an unusual waxiness. It is for this reason that Semillon is the sort of wine that will repay your patience—find a style you like and you'll have a lifelong friend.

WHAT A LOAD OF ROT

There is no doubt that Semillon is the unsung hero of white grapes. In combination with Sauvignon Blanc it is used to make Sauternes, arguably the greatest sweet white wine in the world; one whose flavors respond beautifully to botrytis, the mold that forms when the grapes rot. Semillon plays a similar role in white Bordeaux and also as a partner to Chardonnay in many New World blends.

GOING IT ALONE IN AUSTRALIA

But it is on its own that Semillon really shines. Its recent revival is a good example of how New World wine producers have succeeded in breathing new life into grapes that were previously underexploited and overlooked. While Semillon is often used to make lackluster wines in France, in its spiritual home in Australia's Hunter Valley the grape puts on a virtuoso performance in extraordinarily rich, nutty dry whites, the first taste of which can completely transform one's whole attitude toward white wine. In the cooler areas of Australia, Semillon is used to produce wines with a fresher, grassier character reminiscent of Sauvignon Blanc. With four to five years' aging it becomes even more intriguing and complex.

Although Semillon might have a reputation as the thinking person's Chardonnay, it seems unlikely that the grape will ever have mass appeal. Like Pinot Noir and Riesling, its style can be so inconsistent that for many people the first taste is also the last. But perseverance will pay huge dividends.

TASTE TEST

Try the following taste test and you could find yourself at the start of a lifelong relationship:

- Hunter Valley Semillon + Semillon-based white Bordeaux + Semillon from a cool Australian region such as Tasmania + Australian blend of Chardonnay and Semillon + Sauternes + good-quality Australian Chardonnay + good-quality New Zealand Sauvignon Blanc

Semillon's role in the production of some of the world's greatest sweet wines is explored further in IDEA 4, *Sweet dreams.*

Try another idea...

"When it is young it is simple, charming, and aromatic, but emerges between its fifth and its seventh birthdays as a truly deep, complex, almost waxy wine."
NICHOLAS FAITH

Defining idea...

COMPARE AND CONTRAST

You should now have tasted the Semillon grape in a variety of different incarnations—on its own as either a dry or a sweet wine or blended with Sauvignon Blanc, with which it has a natural affinity. Even if you didn't find a style that you liked, try persevering, particularly with examples from Australia.

How did it go?

Q   Why is Semillon so often associated with Chardonnay despite the fact that these two grapes make wines with such different flavors and aromas?

A   *Partly because it is so often blended with Chardonnay. The other reason is that, like Chardonnay, it is one of Australia's most popular white grapes.*

Q   Why is it that cool areas tend to produce a fresher style of Semillon?

A   *For the same reason that all white wines from cooler areas taste fresher. Because the grapes never become overripe, they have a more vibrant, zingy character.*

Q   I love the nuttiness of some older Semillons. Is this the result of oak aging?

A   *No. With age Semillon develops a wonderfully nutty character all on its own.*

46

Break for the Bordeaux

Bordeaux might be the most complex, confusing wine region in the world, but persevere and you will be rewarded with the most magnificent, subtle wines known to humankind.

Bordeaux is so vast and so sprawling and produces such a vast array of different wines that it is an area about which it's impossible to generalize.

But for many wine lovers that is part of its appeal. Bordeaux is a rich hunting ground that you could spend a lifetime getting to know. To start, it helps to understand a little about its geology, geography, and ludicrously outdated hierarchy. Then you simply need to let your palate loose on its multitude of styles, some good, some deeply disappointing.

THE GEOGRAPHY OF BORDEAUX IN A HUNDRED WORDS

The region is split by the Gironde River. Conveniently, the left-hand side is known as the Left Bank and the right-hand side is known as the Right Bank. The Left Bank

Here's an idea for you... **Because Bordeaux is such a vast and sprawling region, it is important to familiarize yourself with its complex anatomy. Every time you try a wine, plot its place of origin on a map—not only will you begin to understand the geography, you'll also make connections between areas and flavors.**

includes some famous areas such as Medoc, Pauillac, and Margaux that make heavy wines dominated by the Cabernet grape. On the Right Bank are the two well-known areas of St. Emilion and Pomerol, which make lighter Merlot-based wines. In addition to these areas you should also try to locate Sauternes. There are various other areas that eventually you should know about, but for the moment it will suffice that you are familiar with these.

THE GEOLOGY OF BORDEAUX

The reason that Bordeaux has had such a long tradition of creating fabulous wines is that it has the happy combination of well-drained soil that is heated by the Mediterranean and cooled by the Atlantic. However, while it makes great wine, the area is hardly picturesque.

THE PECKING ORDER

Between the 1850s and the 1950s many of Bordeaux's vineyards were classified in a number of different strata. The first classification in 1855—of most of the vineyards on the Left Bank—was carried out at the time of the Exposition Universelle in Paris and still influences wine prices 150 years later. Free-thinking drinkers, however, tend to trust their taste buds rather than ludicrously outdated wine parades.

THE STYLE OF BORDEAUX WINES

- The red wines are made primarily from Cabernet Sauvignon and/or Merlot as well as a smaller proportion of other grapes such as Cabernet Franc, Petit Verdot, and Malbec.
- The best-known sweet wines are made in Sauternes.
- The best-known white wines are made in Graves and Entre-deux-mers.

There's more on the Cabernet grape in all its various incarnations in IDEA 20, *Counting on Cabernet.*

Try another idea...

BORDEAUX VINTAGES

In the same way that free-thinking drinkers ignore classifications, they also don't set much store by vintage charts that rate wines according to the year they were made. Bordeaux is such a vast area with so many producers that it offers a huge variety of styles in any given year. The only dependable gauges of quality are your taste buds and your nose.

BORDEAUX'S PLACE IN THE BRAVE NEW WORLD OF WINE

For years Bordeaux might have traded on its impressive history but in the modern wine world, prestige is not enough to guarantee commercial success; the rise of wine regions such as Australia, Chile, and South Africa means that it is now not enough simply to have the words "Cru Bourgeois" or "Grand Cru Classe" on the label. But it isn't just competition that is

"More than one invalid abandoned by the doctors has been seen to drink the good old wine of Bordeaux."
MEMBERS OF THE JURY judging Bordeaux wine in the 1850s

Defining idea...

205

the problem. Bordeaux has two other major disadvantages; one is that the styles of many of its wines are completely out of sync with contemporary taste; the other is that the region's complex geography and hierarchy make its wines a major turn-off for the new generation of wine drinkers. However, the fact that many people find the region's wines so impenetrable is good news for the free-thinking drinkers— lack of demand will keep prices affordable with the result that the casual wine buyer's loss is our gain.

TASTE TEST—THE REDS

■ Good-quality Cabernet-based red from Medoc + good-quality Merlot-based red from St. Emilion or Pomerol + cheap basic red Bordeaux + good-quality aged Rioja + good-quality Australian Cabernet + good-quality Chilean Merlot

How did the Cabernets and Merlots from Bordeaux compare with those from other parts of the world? Did you detect a similarity among the Bordeaux wines?

TASTE TEST—THE WHITES

■ Cheap white Bordeaux + expensive white Bordeaux + New Zealand Sauvignon Blanc + Australian Semillon

What differences in style did you notice among these wines?

Q **Why is cheap red Bordeaux such bad value compared to inexpensive wines from other parts of the world?**

How did it go?

A *Largely because although the weather in Bordeaux is perfect for painstakingly made, pricey red, it isn't ideal for the production of cheaper wines. If you want cheap reds it makes sense to head for the southern hemisphere.*

Q **Is Bordeaux that is listed in swanky classifications not much good?**

A *On the contrary, the wines in the higher echelons are some of the finest in the world. However, if you want to remain true to your free-thinking drinking principles, you must ignore such hierarchies. Allow yourself to be the judge of a wine's quality, not some long-dead Frenchman.*

Q **Why are many of the Bordeaux whites so thin and mean?**

A *It has to be said that white wine production is not Bordeaux's forte. But don't reject these whites out of hand. You'll find some good-value basic wines and some more expensive, deliciously smoky examples that are fabulous.*

47

Many happy returns?

For some wine buffs, buying wine and selling it a few years later at a profit is a crafty way of helping to fund their drinking habits. Well, that's the theory anyway . . .

On the few occasions that wine hits the news, the story rarely has anything to do with the pleasure that wine offers and instead focuses on its value.

"Record prices paid for magnum of Chateau Something-or-other" is the sort of headline we're used to reading, but it isn't often that a bottle of wine makes the front page because it happens to be astonishingly delicious. For people who genuinely love wine—for the pleasure it gives, the fascination it inspires, the quality it adds to our lives—the idea that it's also a commodity that can be used to turn a fast buck seems a little unsettling. More depressing still is the fact that when some dusty bottle of Sauternes dating back to the Napoleonic Wars goes for thousands of dollars at auction it is not because it is a great wine but simply because it is so very rare that some obsessive collector is prepared to pay a ludicrous price for the pleasure of owning it. However, as well as the big-spending collectors, there's also a subset of wine buffs who try to assuage the guilt they feel about spending money on good wine by making their hobby pay.

Here's an idea for you... **Even if you can make wine investment pay, it relies on you having a love for old wines. Before embarking on the arduous business of buying and selling wines, make sure that you are certain that you are wedded to the flavor and aroma of aged wines. And even if you are, are there qualities in old wines that you might possibly find in less expensive vintages than those from Bordeaux and Burgundy?**

THE FREE WINE THEORY

The theory goes like this. Each year you buy, through a wine merchant, a case of wine—usually red Bordeaux or Burgundy—at a preferential rate from a good vintage before it is bottled (known as buying "en primeur"). When the wine eventually arrives you either leave it in the merchant's cellar or store it in your own. In a few years' time, when the wine has reached maturity, you sell half the wine at a profit, which you use to buy some more wine before it is bottled, and drink the rest.

It sounds simple, doesn't it? But just bear in mind the following pitfalls and hidden costs:

- The price at which the wine is advertised by the producer looks attractive, but by the time it reaches you or the wine merchant it will have attracted taxes that bump up the price.
- If you decide to keep the wine on the merchant's premises you will have to pay a storage charge. There's also a possibility that if the merchant goes bust you could lose all your wine.
- Even if you have enough space with the right conditions for storing wine, there's the chance that it could be stolen or that your cellar could be damaged by a fire or a flood.
- The wine might fail to fulfill its potential and therefore offer little, if any, return on your investment.

Some people further justify buying in this way by pointing out that in some countries the practice can be a very tax-efficient form of investment. However, with so many potential pitfalls and overheads, the risks seem high and

The relationship between wine and age is explored in IDEA 14, *Growing old gracefully.*

Try another idea...

the potential returns slim. Remember, too, that in what are thought to be very good vintages—2000, for example—competition for wines is intense and so prices rise dramatically and offer very little potential for significant returns for many years to come.

CONSIDER THE ALTERNATIVES

Buying wine en primeur and storing it for a few years is not the only way to get your hands on old vintage wine. By the time you have paid for the wine and all the additional cost of duty and storage (and accounted for the fact that your money has been tied up for a few years) buying older vintages from a wine merchant doesn't seem quite so expensive. Another possibility is to buy old wine at auction—however, this is more complicated and there can be greater risks involved. The other advantage to buying wines in this way is that it gives you the option to choose the wine you want to drink—rather than something that you happened to buy a few years before that might not have performed particularly well.

"You don't get owt for nowt."
OLD NORTHERN ENGLISH SAYING

Defining idea...

211

How did it go?

Q   **You paint a very grim picture of wine investment. Is it really not possible to make serious money out of wine?**

A   *If you are prepared to take risks and do plenty of research it should be possible to make a return. But, as in buying and selling shares, there's a chance that your profits will be slim—or, worse still, you could lose money.*

Q   **Is it only Bordeaux and Burgundy that increase in value?**

A   *No. Other classic European wines can appreciate, as can a few from the southern hemisphere. But remember that any wine—like anything—is only worth what someone else is prepared to pay for it.*

Q   **What should I do if I come across old bottles of wine that could be of value?**

A   *Start by looking for their names on the Internet. If they show up, try to find out how much they are being sold for. Alternatively, talk to the staff at an auction house or specialist dealer. Remember that auction houses will charge a commission. Even if the wines are good, it might make more sense to drink them up.*

48

Beyond Liebfraumilch

Most of us have so many negative misconceptions about German wine that only a blind tasting can offer any objectivity. But first you must seek some professional help.

It is easy to write off German wines. For many of us, our first taste of them has—quite understandably—been our last.

Thin, mean, and tasteless, in the '70s poor quality German wines fueled institutional functions, where their only attraction appeared to be that they were cold and wet— and very, very cheap. But it's easy to understand how they became so popular. Thirty years ago the world of wine was a very different place. The Australians were still making sweet reds for local consumption, sanctions hampered the export of South African wine, and Chile's economy was in disarray. What were the options? In that era Bordeaux, Burgundy, Sancerre, and Pouilly Fumé were beyond the pockets of most consumers, much of the output of southern France was undrinkable cooperative produce, and Italian producers were swamping the market with thin, tasteless Lambrusco, Soave, and Valpolicella. In that context, Germany's wines seemed relatively attractive. Served teeth-chatteringly cold, they seemed just about palatable.

Here's an idea for you... **Rather than serving Champagne before a meal, try offering a good dry Riesling as an alternative. Its assertive style is perfect for stimulating the appetite—and it's much cheaper. On the whole, dry Riesling is better enjoyed on its own than with food. Sweeter styles can make good dessert wines.**

MORE BAD NEWS

But poor quality is just one of Germany's catalog of woes. In the brave new wine world where the fashion is for dry styles of wines with a hint of fruitiness and with labels that are easy to understand, the idiosyncratic style of many German wines and their ludicrous gradations of style and quality and austere-looking labels make them a marketing executive's nightmare. However energetically one might trumpet the revival of interest in Riesling, most consumers still remember their first taste of German wine and opt instead for the sunny flavors of Chardonnay.

It gets worse. In the same way that they have exploited classic French grapes such as Sauvignon Blanc, Shiraz, Semillon, Cabernet, and, of course, Chardonnay, New World winemakers have also succeeded in making Riesling with greater appeal and approachability than have winemakers in its spiritual home.

A LITTLE HELP FROM YOUR FRIENDS

Free-thinking drinkers don't give a fig about the whims of fashion—or something as trifling as an ugly, incomprehensible bottle. But, equally, they don't want their path to vinous nirvana to be hampered by a wine region that amounts to one giant red herring. Don't even try to master the litany of Tafelwein, Landwein, QbA, and QmPs. Instead, enlist the help of a wine merchant. If there's one thing that wine merchants love, it's an underdog—and at the top of their list of underdogs is Germany. For very nerdy wine merchants, one of the great attractions of German winemaking is its impenetrability. They will love showing off their intimate knowledge of the subject, so use it.

If you enjoyed the idiosyncratic style of German Riesling, explore other wines with similar qualities in IDEA 9, Whites with attitude.

Try another idea...

TASTE TEST

In the interests of weeding out it is essential that you limit yourself initially to just one grape: Riesling. Ask your friendly merchant to suggest wines that fit the following descriptions and then compare them against each other.

■ Cheap German Riesling + good-quality dry German Riesling + good-quality medium sweet German Riesling + good-quality dry Australian Riesling + good-quality expensive New Zealand Riesling + Sauternes + inexpensive Australian Chardonnay

COMPARE AND CONTRAST

Stripped of their off-putting labels—and your preconceptions—consider the styles of the wines in front of you. If at first you find the flavors a little offbeat, imagine drinking them in a variety of different situations—perhaps with Asian food or ice cold on a summer evening. The more you immerse yourself in their flavors, the less alien they will seem.

"A German wine label is one thing that life's too short for, a daunting testimony to that peculiar nation's love of details and organization."
KINGSLEY AMIS

Defining idea...

Q   Why do Australian and New Zealand Riesling usually have a slightly richer style than Riesling from Germany?

A   *Like the difference between so many European and New World wines, this comes down partly to winemaking and partly to the weather. But the more you taste, the more you might find that what German Rieslings lack in weight they more than make up for in elegance and complexity.*

Q   In some of the older Rieslings I tried—from both Germany and the New World—I thought I noticed a somewhat oily aroma. Am I imagining it?

A   *No. One of the multitude of alluring aromas that Riesling offers is an unusual smell like the one you describe. It's been compared to everything from "pencil shavings" to "gasoline."*

Q   Why does good-quality German Riesling tend to be such good value for the money?

A   *Because such are the misconceptions about German wine that nobody other than rabid wine enthusiasts is prepared to buy it.*

49

Local heroes

Some of the best wines have an extra dimension: As well as being delicious they also express the winemaking tradition of the area where they were made. And the best needn't cost a fortune.

How should a good wine taste? "Fabulous" is the obvious answer. If only it were so simple!

Wine falls into two categories: the stuff that reflects the winemaking tradition of the region where it was produced and the sort that tastes as though it could have been made anywhere in the world where the sun shines enough to ripen grapes. There's not much wrong with the latter; the huge advances in winemaking technology in the last decade have made it possible to produce good-value wines virtually anywhere. What sets these two kinds of wine apart is something that wine buffs call "typicity"—meaning that they conform to a certain style that is typical of the wine's birthplace. How important is this quality? If wine is enjoyable to drink, surely to worry about typicity is nothing more than splitting hairs? Possibly. But a world without wines that reflect their origins would be very boring.

Here's an idea for you...

Typical wines tend to be part of a gastronomic tradition. Try drinking wines that are typical of an area with corresponding regional specialities, e.g., bold southern French red with cassoulet and Muscadet with seafood.

When it comes to wine, variety is undoubtedly the spice of life. While the consistency of "global" wines might offer a convenient option for everyday drinking, the highs and lows are provided by wines that taste of the place they come from. There are parallels between winemaking and food. The people of every region of the world have their own tastes in food that are influenced by the available ingredients, the climate, and the gastronomic tradition that has evolved over the years. Precisely the same is true of wine.

A SENSE OF PLACE VERSUS A SUGGESTION OF TERROIR

Describing a wine as having a "sense of place" could easily be confused with suggesting that it expresses terroir. Though terroir does contribute to the sense of place, the typicity of a wine has more to do with winemaking tradition—the style of wine created by techniques such as oak aging and blending. The grim reapers of the wine world might make gloomy predictions that typical wines are being replaced with ones that have no regional characteristics, but the fact is that these two kinds of wine can coexist happily side by side.

TASTE TEST—REDS

To distinguish between these two kinds of wine, try comparing the following:

■ Inexpensive Chilean Merlot + good-quality Rioja

TASTE TEST—WHITES

■ Inexpensive Chilean Sauvignon Blanc + good-quality Sancerre

Terroir is a quality that contributes to the typicity of a wine. There's more discussion of this subject in IDEA 17, *The reign of terroir*.

Try another idea...

COMPARE AND CONTRAST

In each case, ask yourself which of the two wines in the glasses before you could have been made anywhere in the world and which has an idiosyncratic feel that is all its own.

WHERE TO FIND TYPICAL WINES

Although it is easy to see typicity as a quality that is peculiar to European wine regions such as France, Italy, and Spain, some New World areas are developing their own styles and winemaking traditions. For instance, Sauvignon Blanc from Marlborough in New Zealand tastes very different from Sauvignon from Western Australia, and Barossa Shiraz has a style different from Shiraz made in South Africa. Here are areas where you are likely to find more typical wines that are true to local tradition than homogenous "global wine."

"No one escapes from his individuality."
ARTHUR SCHOPENHAUER

Defining idea...

OLD WORLD	**THE NEW WORLD**
Bordeaux	The Barossa Valley
Burgundy	The Clare Valley
The Loire	The Hunter Valley
The Mosel Valley	The Margaret River
Rioja	The Napa Valley
The South of France	Sonoma
Tuscany	

How did it go?

Q   Is it coincidental that two of the wines in the taste test are from Chile?

A   *No—although they could have been from almost any region. While Chile now makes some fantastic high-quality wines it also produces many "global wines" that taste as though they could come from almost anywhere in the world.*

Q   Do all expensive wines have a sense of place?

A   *Not necessarily. Typicity is not related to price. There are plenty of cheap and expensive wines that don't have any local characteristics.*

Q   Is it true that with "global wines" you at least know what you're going to get?

A   *Yes. A basic Chardonnay from Chile is likely to taste pretty much like one from South Africa or Australia. Typical wines are likely to be far less consistent—but finding a good one more than repays the effort.*

50

Keeping your palate on its toes

Even when you're focusing on a limited number of grape varieties and styles, it's useful to venture occasionally into uncharted territory.

In order to understand wine you need to initially cull the number of wines you focus on down to a manageable selection. But in doing this you will only scratch the surface of the huge range of styles and grapes that are offered.

Even on the first leg of the path to vinous nirvana, it is important to expose your palate to other styles of wine without letting them cloud your understanding. There are a huge number of wines that no one except a few hardened wine buffs are aware of. Plenty of wines are made purely for local consumption, such as Austrian Gruner Veltliner, Swiss Chasselas, Italian Aglianico, Uruguayan Tannat, and Canadian Ice Wine. Though initially you should keep these wines at arm's length, they will eventually be essential for pushing your taste buds to the extremes—just as the best fitness training program will exercise muscles that you don't normally use. The chances are that you won't like them. But even if you don't they will offer

Here's an idea for you...

Good sources of unusual wines are restaurants that specialize in offbeat cuisine such as German, Lebanese, or Swiss. Good Greek, Cypriot, and Turkish restaurants also tend to have a wide selection of wines from the Mediterranean. Most of these specialist restaurants are likely to have wines that it would be difficult to buy anywhere else. These restaurants will also give you the opportunity to taste the wines in a gastronomic context in which they might not taste quite so weird.

flavors and aromas that your palate and nose wouldn't otherwise be subjected to. They will stretch your senses to the extremes of their experience.

The secret to tasting offbeat wines is never to get too involved. You don't need to know a great deal about wine in order to enjoy it. It doesn't really matter whether Gruner Veltliner, Tannat, Aglianico, or Eiswein is a grape or a style of wine. Nor does it really matter whether they come from Austria, Uruguay, Italy, or Canada. What is far more important is that you, your palate, and your nose are receptive to them. Of course, when—or if—you find an offbeat wine that you like, that might be the time to investigate the winemaking tradition from which it springs.

WHERE TO SEEK THE WEIRD AND WONDERFUL

Although wine is made everywhere from Austria to Zimbabwe, many of the more obscure winemaking regions are devoted to classic French varieties such as Cabernet and Chardonnay. For some really extreme experiences, try wines made from local grape varieties.

- **Austria** Gruner Veltliner might twist the tongue, but its taste should also keep it on its toes.

- **England** English wines may not be to everyone's taste, but varieties such as Seyval Banc, Schonburger, Huxelrebe, Bacchus, Kerner, and Ortega can't fail to stimulate the palate.

- **Germany** Plenty of strangers here. Try Scheurebe Silvaner, Lemberger, and Dornfelder.

- **Greece** Ignore the new generation of modern wines and try the native Greek varieties such as Agiorgitiko.

- **Mexico** Try the fabulous, obscure Petite Sirah grape, which will put predictable Cabernet to shame.

- **Switzerland** Go with local specialities such as Chasselas, Arvine, and Amigne.

If offbeat wines strike your fancy, try IDEA 9, *Whites with attitude*, and IDEA 40, *Simply reds*. For a discussion of whether grape varieties are important see IDEA 10, *Grape expectations*.

Try another idea...

"One should try everything once, except incest and folk dancing."
SIR ARNOLD BAX

Defining idea...

223

HOW FOOD CAN HELP

When tasting unusual wines such as these, start by doing so in a formal way, noting the flavor, aroma, and color so that you are able to make as objective a judgment as possible. However, having done so, it is essential that you have food on hand; few wines are created to be sampled in the formal environment of a tasting. The best option is a dish from the wine's country of origin—for example Chasselas with fondue, Mexican Petite Sirah with chili, and Agiorgitiko with a lamb kebab. It is remarkable how wines taste completely different when experienced in the context of the gastronomic tradition in which they were produced—it also explains why wines might taste delicious in their country of origin but strangely alien once you return home.

How did it go?

Q   I was amazed by some of the wines that I've come across—notably those from Greece. Why is it so difficult to buy offbeat wines outside the country where they're made?

A   *Simply because there are already so many wines that appeal to the majority of wine drinkers. However, Greek wines are becoming more commonplace on the export market and a couple of Lebanese wineries have established international reputations.*

Q   Why is it that Morocco and Algeria, wine regions that are so close to France, haven't had much success with wine production?

A   *There have been vast improvements in both country's wines and they are being exported. Algerian wines have actually been exported for years—albeit in a rather covert way: they often ended up in France, where they were blended with poor local vintages and passed off as French.*

51

Avoiding the revenge of Bacchus

Hangovers are the scourge of every enthusiastic drinker. But because there's no such thing as a hangover cure the most sensible approach is avoidance.

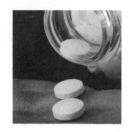

There are treatments that will make you feel slightly less grim than you did before taking them—or will replace one disgusting taste in your mouth with another.

But so far no one has come up with anything that will make you feel as good as you would after an alcohol-free evening and plenty of sleep. The whole point of a hangover is that it's a punishment. As a child you learned that if you ate too much you'd be sick or that if you put your hand near fire you'd get burned. In the same way, those who drink too much are rewarded with a throbbing head, sluggish metabolism, and a mouth that feels like the bottom of a hamster's cage. Their bodies are saying, "Don't do it again!"

For the free-thinking drinker, wine is not about intoxication—it's about appreciating subtle flavors and aromas. Nevertheless, a gastronomic blowout that involves matching diverse foods to diverse wines is likely to wreak havoc with your system.

Here's an
idea for
you...

Many wine buffs keep a few bottles of wine open at the same time—partly so that they can compare them and also so that they can try them out with different foods. On a day-to-day basis this habit can encourage you to simply taste a couple of wines rather than open a bottle and finish it within a day or two.

THE FREE-THINKING DRINKER'S GUIDE TO HANGOVER AVOIDANCE

If you're taking part in a gastronomic session that involves matching different wines with different courses, make sure that you don't drink more than half a glass of each (wine buffs prefer half-filled glasses anyway because they provide a greater distance between the surface of the wine and your nose, allowing aromas to circulate). Remember, too, that to enjoy a wine you don't need to drink a huge quantity of it—just enough to savor.

Plenty of water is essential—partly because it acts as a brake on the amount of wine that you can drink and partly because it counters the diuretic effect of alcohol. Try to drink a couple of large glasses of water before you get anywhere near an aperitif. This avoids the peril of using wine to quench your thirst. For this purpose, still water is ideal. Fizzy water can bloat you and discourage you from drinking enough of it. Your goal should be to drink at least a large glass of water for every small glass of wine you drink. As you'll know from the taste tests, water is a good way of cleansing your palate in preparation for the next wine.

The better the wines you drink, the less likely you are to feel the consequences the morning after (there's no clinical evidence for this, just the testaments of millions of well-seasoned drinkers). The other advantage of good-quality wine is that it tends to be more satisfying, so you aren't tempted to drink more than you need.

KNOWING WHEN TO STOP

For a sobering warning about the consequences of alcohol abuse, turn to IDEA 35, *On doctor's orders.*

Try another idea...

The mark of a serial binger is someone who can't make that Pavlovian connection between excessive drinking and the physical pain experienced the morning after. Just remember that your memory of a good meal will be enhanced if it isn't clouded by hazy recollections of its later stages the morning after. Much of the damage is done in the last throes of a meal. Try to avoid the following:

- **Coffee.** Alcohol does enough to disrupt your sleep patterns. Why make the situation even worse?
- **More than one glass of Port.** Either drink Port when you are sober or drink it sparingly if you are mildly drunk. It might go down easily but it has an alcohol content of 19 percent.
- **Spirits.** Is the end of a meal really the time to enjoy your prized single malt? If anything, it should be deployed as an early-evening aperitif when you aren't planning to do much drinking.

A NOTE ON HABITUAL DRINKING

"My view is that the golden rule in life is never to have too much of anything."
TERENCE

Defining idea...

Much more dangerous than the occasional binge is developing a pattern of habitual drinking. Even those who consider themselves moderate drinkers find it hard to pass an evening without drinking at least one or two glasses of wine—a number that can all too easily increase to three or four. From this seemingly manageable intake it is easy to slip into a bottle a day habit—

particularly at times of stress. The only way to avoid this is to ensure that wine consumption doesn't become a habit. Whenever possible try to avoid drinking for two days in succession and make sure that when you drink it is in company rather than alone. Often, when you feel that you need a glass of wine in the early evening it isn't alcohol that you're yearning for but water—try to drink a couple of large glasses of water and see whether the urge passes.

How did it go?

Q Are there really no effective hangover cures?

A   *At best, they are palliative. Rather than putting money and effort into trying to cure a hangover, it's better to avoid getting one in the first place.*

Q Aren't coffee and digestifs a good way to settle the stomach?

A   *That's one way of looking at it. Remember that the traditional ingredients of the gastronomic blowouts, from aperitifs and amuse geules to coffee and petit fours, were created for people who didn't have to get up for work the next day.*

52

Have you achieved vinous nirvana?

Simply following my advice and trying the taste tests won't guarantee that you'll become a free-thinking drinker in a flash. But if you persist you'll be handsomely rewarded with a lifetime of pleasure.

It won't happen overnight. You'll taste hundreds of wines and still think that some are good because they have a prestigious name on the label—or bad because they are cheap.

However, the more that you taste, the more you'll begin to trust your own instincts. You'll begin to realize that some expensive wines can taste like battery acid and some cheap wines like nectar. Even when this happens, it will be your own secret. You'll think it, even be fairly convinced of it, but you won't dare to make your opinions known. Then one day you'll pull the cork on a bottle of obscure or little-loved wine, taste it, love it, and—most importantly—shout your enthusiasm from the rooftops without fear of embarrassment. You'll be prepared to stand up and be counted. That is the hallmark of vinous nirvana. This new dimension to your

Here's an idea for you... **Start testing your opinions on someone who was at the same stage you were at before you embarked on your present exploration of wine. Pour a glass of a well-known wine (be sure to make its identity clear) and ask her to talk about it. Compare what she has to say with your own thoughts. Haven't you come a long way?**

appreciation of wine will enable you to drink it without fear of embarrassment and to feel confident in saying that it's good, bad, or corked.

TELLTALE SIGNS THAT YOU'VE BECOME A FREE-THINKING DRINKER

1. You don't immediately huff and puff with appreciation when someone pours you a glass from a fancy bottle of wine.

2. You serve unusual, offbeat wines with confidence.

3. You question the opinions of wine buffs, wine merchants, and sommeliers.

4. You express your opinions with the same confidence you would when talking about any other subject you know a lot about.

5. Your decisions to serve certain wines with different sorts of food are based on your own experience rather than what you have read in a book—or on the back of the bottle.

However, the more you know about wine, the greater the danger that you might fall into the same trap into which other wine enthusiasts have fallen—that you become more interested in the detail than in the bigger picture.

FIVE SIGNS THAT YOU'RE BECOMING A BORE

1. You develop an unhealthy interest in the way that wine is made.

2. You start buying tickets to vertical tastings that allow you to compare the differences between a range of vintages of the same wine.

3. You become obsessed with a wine's failings rather than its attractions.

4. You come up with phrases such as "Wow, get a load of that yeasty autolysis."

5. You become more interested in experts' opinions rather than your own.

Free-thinking drinking is not about taking wine lightly; it is simply about not letting your instincts be clouded by issues that don't matter. Try to remember the joy you felt when you first tasted a wine and found it truly delicious. How much did that pleasure have to do with your knowledge of how or where it was made? The secret to vinous nirvana is more about what you feel than what you know.

WHERE NEXT?

This is just the beginning. Having taken the fear out of wine you can now conquer just about any vinous subject. You have enough knowledge to be able to place almost any wine, however obscure, in context. And if your knowledge of a particular wine is patchy,

If you need reminding of the extent to which the uninitiated labor under misconceptions, turn to IDEA 1, *Never mind the bollocks.* Then consider how much you have come to rely on your own opinions rather than what others want you to believe.

Try another idea...

"The palate, like the eye, the ear, or touch, acquires with practice various degrees of sensitiveness that would be incredible were it not well ascertained fact."
T. G. SHAW

Defining idea...

there is nothing that you won't find between the covers of a good wine encyclopedia. Understanding wine is like joining dots to make a picture—the more you connect, the clearer the picture will become. What is important, too, is always to have an atlas on hand; when you can pinpoint the origin of wine it becomes more than just a liquid in a glass. A wine with an origin becomes an expression of the landscape and winemaking tradition in which it was produced and wine appreciation becomes a form of armchair travel. Suddenly, even an expensive bottle of wine seems like a bargain.

How did it go?

Q   Is there anything intrinsically wrong with becoming a wine bore?

A   No, they serve a useful purpose in that they have helped to increase the overall quality of wine. However, there is a danger that you'll miss out on much of the enjoyment of wine by focusing on matters that are not essential to the sensual enjoyment of wine.

Q   How does one avoid becoming a wine bore?

A   Limit the amount that you read about wine and try as much as you can to drink wine in the context of a meal rather than a formal tasting environment. Wine is there to be enjoyed.

Where it's at . . .

Index

52 Brilliant Ideas

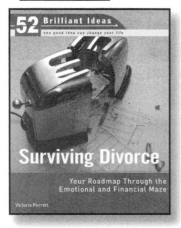

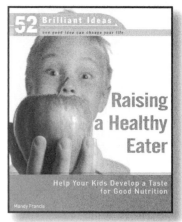

SURVIVING DIVORCE
978-0-399-53305-1

SLEEP DEEP
978-0-399-53323-5

CULTIVATE A COOL CAREER
978-0-399-53338-9

LIVE LONGER
978-0-399-53302-0

UNLEASH YOUR CREATIVITY
978-0-399-53325-9

RAISING A HEALTHY EATER
978-0-399-53339-6

PERIGEE An imprint of Penguin Group (USA)

one good idea can change your life

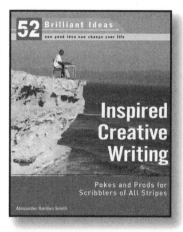
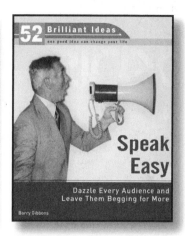